SPECIALTIES
OF
THE
HOUSE .. YOUR HOUSE!

Have you ever eaten at Maxims in Paris, or any of the really fabulous places whose specialties are as tempting to look at as they are to eat?

Elsie Lee's EASY GOURMET COOKING is a rare and unique collection of these very special recipies—that you can prepare in your own home. From subtle and exotic Oriental dishes to the superb cuisine of the Mediterranean, they are all here—designed to make the simplest table elegant and please the most discriminating palates.

Your friends will be delighted and you will probably be amazed—because these delicious recipies are easy to understand, and easy to cook, too. A shopping guide (where and how to buy some very special ingredients) has been included for your convenience, plus a variety of culinary secrets gleaned from years of experience by the best chefs of the world.

EASY GOURMET COOKING

by Elsie Lee

PRESTIGE BOOKS · NEW YORK

**PRESTIGE BOOKS INC. • 18 EAST 41ST STREET
NEW YORK, N.Y. 10017**

Copyright 1962 by Elsie Lee

ONTENTS

CHAPTER 1

QUICK TIPS TO QUICK COOKERY

These days, nothing is more fun—nor more socially acceptable—than "messing about in the kitchen." What with pressure cookers, electric broilers and blenders, packaged mixes, bottled sauces, every possible herb or spice from the Indies, and something new every day in the frozen food section of any supermarket, *Cookery* is the latest game, the newest fad.

Now that women find it's fun to cook, and men are remembering that every great name in gastronomy from Epicurus to Escoffier is masculine, the next step is Gourmet Cookery —and turning yourself into a Cordon Bleu is no longer difficult.

In this book we present a selection of great traditional dishes, as well as some "novelties." All are designed to be prepared in a limited time for the modern-day reproduction of a Lucullan Feast—and all are proportioned for *four* hungry gourmets. Note, too, that all gourmet recipes are intended for adults—because a child's palate does not develop until the late teens.

Even ten years ago, many of these recipes could not have been included, and there is no denying that some great culinary masterpieces still cannot be prepared in only thirty minutes. Even with a pressure cooker, the true Coq au Vin, Blanquette de Veau or Boeuf BourguigNonne, while edible cannot possess the suave blend of flavors that comes from leisurely simmering.

Time is essential, too, for chilling or resting of some dishes that can easily be prepared in a few minutes. Therefore, a few recipes are included that require 30 minutes or less to prepare—but which must be allowed to stand overnight before the final minutes or preparation and service.

These are marked Two-Step Cookery; neither step requires more than 30 minutes—but if you like to think this a quibble, we can only recommend that you try the dish and hope it will be found worthy of inclusion.

BASIC TIPS TO THE CHEF

1. It may actually be easier to prepare a glamorous dish (foreign name and all), than the run-of-the-mill dishes you've been eating all your life.

2. Read all the way through a recipe first; check to be sure ingredients are at hand. You will save time and achieve better results if you understand, in general terms, what you are going to do before you start to do it.

3. Never try to make more than one unfamiliar recipe for the same meal! A wise chef never tries a new recipe when there is "company," either. Always get the recipe under your belt at least once before you attempt to produce it with *eclat* for strangers.

4. Accurate measurements are essential; accurate timing is essential. Never hesitate to make your personal penciled comments next to the recipe; the annotated cookbook is a chef's most valuable possession.

5. Gourmet cookery requires the *best* quality in ingredients. Please, no substitutions! Real butter, real cream, the freshest mushrooms, the best olive oil . . . all are essential for a *gourmet* dish.

6. When there are 4 or 6 people for dinner, the chef dictates the schedule: Finish the drinks, wash the hands, and sit down! But for more than 6 people (even if they will be formally seated at the table), it's wise to plan a main dish that can only improve with overcooking!

7. *Wipe* meats, poultry and fish on paper toweling, rather than washing—and *never* season before cooking, as this toughens the flesh. Seasonings go into sauces, or should be added at the end of the plain-cooking.

8. Spaghetti sauces, curries and stews are easy ways to use up leftovers—the easiest things to stretch for unexpected guests—and the simplest things to prepare when the cook wants to enjoy the fun as well as set a distinguished meal on the table.

GO-TOGETHERS AND SUBSTITUTES

1. Any recipe requiring: green pepper, scallions, celery, mushrooms, tomatoes or parsley, may be amplified or extended by adding an equal amount of any of the others.

2. Shrimp, crab, scallops and lobsters respond to a rich sauce of cream, white wine and mushrooms, plus a dash of nutmeg—or thin tart lemon-butter-parsley sauces . . . but oysters, clams and mussels prefer the thin sauce.

3. Salted or corned meats are exclusive and do not combine happily with anything but chicken and eggs. All other plain-cooked meats and poultry can be teamed for a chef's salad, a potluck curry, sliced meat platter, or creamed in patty shells.

4. In a *dire* emergency, chicken creamed or curried can be stretched by a tin of white meat tuna. Cut the oil with lemon juice, douse in cold water, and slice into neat pieces.

5. Yoghurt and sour cream are interchangeable—although the flavor will be slightly different in the final dish.

6. Use condensed cream soups for a quick white sauce: MBT soup packets are quicker to use than pressed bouillon or consomme cubes. Dilute cream soups ⅔ to ¾ when used as a sauce. For dishes with plenty of cooking liquid, sprinkle powders directly into hot liquid and stir gently until dissolved.

SAUCES

The saying goes (although it's a gross libel today) that "The French have a hundred sauces to disguise a few foods —and the Americans have a hundred foods disguised only by White Sauce!"

It is true that many great gourmet dishes involve a special sauce, which used to take hours to prepare. For the quick gourmet chef, there's a way around this:

1. *Hollandaise and Bearnaise:* Both are available in glass jars. If you cannot find them in your local gourmet shop, consult the listing at the end of this chapter.

2. *Madeira, Armoricaine, Newburg, Supreme, et al:* These,

too, are available tinned or frozen, and will transform the humble hamburger or leftover into a gourmet's dream.

3. *Bottled Meat Sauces:* Heinz A-1, H-P, Escoffier's Diable, Robert or Cumberland sauce, Worcestershire, and a wide range of mustards from Devilled to Bahamian to Dijon— Wash your hands thoroughly, use a judicious few tablespoons of whatever you fancy, and rub it thoroughly into chops and steaks. This replaces the *marinades* which used to take hours.

4. *Dessert Sauces:* Be cautious about these! There are lots of edible varieties—but very few that come up to a gourmet's standard! Escoffier's Sauce Melba, and General Foods Gourmet Fudge Sauce Royale are acceptable . . . but as you will see in Chapter 13, there are innumerable quick tricks with liqueurs and fresh fruit for presenting gourmet desserts in a minute.

5. *Basting Sauces:* Here you begin to be a gourmet chef, for a basting sauce is largely invention based on experience as you grow proficient with recipes.

Basting sauces are used with fish, meat and poultry. Generally, they are melted butter blended with herbs—or spices —or fruit and fruit peels—with or without a dash of cooking wine. The precise ingredients depend upon the final flavor desired: tangy, sultry, or sweetish.

The basting sauce should be made at the start of the cooking operation, placed over the lowest possible heat, allowed to sit and grow acquainted with itself. A quarter pound of butter makes an adequate basting sauce; half a pound is sometimes better—if you can bring yourself to it!

The basic procedure is to combine butter chunks and desired seasonings or flavorings in a small saucepot (a stainless steel one-cup measure with a handle is satisfactory), and to obtain the full savory blend by simmering gently during the first steps of searing meat or poultry, firming the fish flesh, etc. A basting sauce is used to moisten and flavor a dish *during* its cooking; it is brushed directly onto roasting meat or poultry with a pastry brush at 10 or 15 minute intervals, or poured over fish and broiled dishes every 5 minutes for quick cookery.

For long cooking roasts, when the basting sauce has all

10

been used, a roaster-baster will pick up pan juices for moistening the dish.

6. *Wine Sauces:* American wines are as good—and often better—than imported brands for cookery. "The better the wine, the better the dish" is the gourmet standard . . . although it's not necessary to buy fine vintage drinking wines for use in the kitchen.

Never buy cooking wine or liquor purely on a price basis; the cheap brands do not have sufficient alcoholic content to create a *flambee* dish—and will not have enough flavor to remain in the sauce. White wines can be used for any recipes, but red wines can only be used for dark meats . . . when they will not discolor the dish.

At table, the only standard today is flavor, and red or white wines are served interchangeably.

When wine is added directly to a dish during cooking, lower the heat *immediately* or the meat will toughen.

7. *Fats and Oils:* For true gourmet cookery, there is *no substitute* for butter unless particularly specified. Sweet butter is preferable, because the amount of salt varies in commercial brands; if salt butter is used, decrease the amount of salt in a recipe and check seasoning just before you serve.

Butter is absolutely essential for sauces and basting, but cannot be used for frying; at high temperatures, it decomposes chemically and burns.

For Deep-Fat Frying, use liquid or hydrogenated oils such as Wesson, Crisco, Spry, etc. These can be re-used once or twice, if you allow sediment to settle and decant (pour off) the clear top fat after each frying. Once frying fat has been used for fish, it cannot be used for anything else! If you enjoy fried foods, it's wise to have two fat kettles—one for fish, and one for everything else.

For all Italian, Spanish or Latin-American dishes, a tablespoon of *olive oil* can replace butter in starting the dish.

Lard is excellent for greasing baking potatoes or pan-frying fish. It cannot be re-used, but is inexpensive enough to discard and start fresh next time.

Bacon grease is equally good for baking potatoes or to saute fish, and can be smeared thickly over chicken breasts

11

or squab before roasting. Because of its positive flavor, only tangy herbs will combine with it for added taste.

If you have time to melt it, or can buy it in jars, *chicken fat* also has many uses, either to baste poultry or (solidified) in place of half the butter required for pastry doughs.

No *gourmet* cook ever uses margarine for anything.

8. *Meat Glazes:* For a handsome browned surface to meat or poultry, mix a tablespoon of commercial gravy coloring such as Kitchen Bouquet, Gravymaster, etc. with two tablespoons of water. Paint all exposed parts of the poultry or meat before placing in the oven.

9. *Shallots* are a small onion bulb resembling garlic in formation of cloves, but very mild in flavor. Typically French, they are not always available but make all the difference in a sauce if they can be had. Minced scallions (spring onions) are an acceptable substitute—and in moments of stress, a tablespoon of grated white onion will equal 2 minced shallots.

10. Grated orange and lemon peel are readily available in jars; a teaspoon equals the grated rind of a whole medium-sized fruit.

11. Garlic can be bought powdered (a quarter teaspon equals a fresh clove), but a garlic press will produce a much better flavor from a peeled garlic clove—if you can afford the time.

Onion and garlic juice are also available; use them purely for flavoring, as many dishes are better with sauteed pieces of onion. Onion flakes are good for home-cooking, but not sufficient for gourmet results.

INGREDIENTS

Despite the immense and satisfying variety of foods in the United States, not everything is equally available everywhere.

Frozen sweetbreads exist on the West Coast, for instance —but are mysteriously not to be had in the East; frozen trout are generally cheaper in the East than in the West; snowpeas are often available in average Western supermarkets, but can only be found in Chinese sections of Eastern cities, and so on.

Meat varies enormously, both in cut and price. Generally speaking, the West Coast has little understanding of meat "extras," and veal kidneys, sweetbreads, tripe and calves' brains are far cheaper there than in the East . . . but the thin pounded veal slices for scallopini are relatively harder to find in the West than in the East. Mutton chops are also unknown to the West—but none too easy to procure in the East, either!

Western lobsters do not possess claws—but abalone is unknown in the East. There is no state of the union that does not contain some sort of local fresh-caught fish, but far too many people seem not to know how good a fish dish can taste.

For the lucky people who live in rural areas with their own vegetable gardens (how we envy them!), there are tiny, fresh garden greens unknown to city dwellers.

So everything is available somewhere—but a gourmet cook learns to use what is freshly available in his own locality. Perhaps there will be some recipes you cannot try because the makings are not at hand—but take heart! Unquestionably, there will be some dishes you can do superbly, which will be impossible for cooks in other parts of the country.

Nearly every community has a store catering to the new interest in gourmet foods; most supermarkets have a fancy food department. If you still cannot find what you need, write to any of the following for an order catalog:

CAVIARTERIA, 153 West 57th Street, New York 19
CHARLES & CO., 340 Madison Avenue, New York City
GOURMET TREATS, 52 West 72nd Street, New York City
JURGENSEN'S, 409 North Beverly Drive, Beverly Hills, Calif.
MAISON GLASS, 52 West 58th Street, New York City
MARYLAND GOURMET MARKET, 414 Amsterdam Avenue, New York City
VENDOME, 15 East 48th Street, New York City

LAST WORDS

Meal-planning can be a terrible trap for the unwary. A gourmet menu must be considered *as a whole;* each course is a subtle bridge between all others; each flavor should be separate, yet blend with everything else; wine is used as an accent to clear the palate.

In the excitement of mastering gourmet-cookery, do not go overboard, and create an end product of indigestion for all!

1. The *theme* of the meal depends on the main dish; other courses should support this. If East Indian curry is the entree, do not precede it by Italian antipasto—or follow with crêpes Suzette!

2. Emphasize *one* course, and simplify all others so they will point up the masterpiece.

3. Never serve more than one rich sauce within the same course. A Chateaubriand with Sauce Bearnaise does *not* team with Broccoli Hollandaise, although this will be wonderful with plain broiled hamburger.

4. Salad is used to clear the palate, in preparation for the final sweet dessert. Following a richly sauced main dish, serve a plain salad with tart dressing—and because salad is basically used in this way by gourmets, wine is *never* served with it.

5. Learn to think of food in its colors: green peas, red tomatoes, white fish, yellow squash, and so on. No gourmet cook would schedule creamed cauliflower with mashed potatoes and boiled codfish, for no amount of paprika or minced parsley could relieve the general colorless appearance.

Think, too, of the color of china, tablecloth, candles and flowers; gourmet cooks *display* a delicious dish to advantage . . . red tomatoes in a white dish, lettuce in a brown wooden bowl, white mashed potatoes against pink roses . . .

6. Some foods (spinach, asparagus, broccoli) are always watery; French fried foods grow soggy in contact with plate juices; noodles, mashed potatoes and such acquire added savor from meat sauce. A gourmet cook considers which foods may be combined on one dinner plate—and which should be served at the side, such as Asparagus Hollandaise.

7. No matter how small the apartment, get the guests on their feet and away from the dinner table after the dessert course! If you like to be lazy over coffee and liqueurs, serve

hem elsewhere (even if only three feet from the table; the ntire effect of a delicious meal is dissipated by sitting too ong over the remnants. Furthermore, even this small movement will prevent torpidity as an aftermath of good food, and llow everyone to digest, feel good, and sparkle conversaionally.

CHAPTER 2

CANAPES AND APPETIZER:

THE FREE LUNCH, or canapes

The expression "free lunch" originated in Victorian saloon —when immense platters of excellent cold meats, potate salad and cheeses were strategically placed along a bar to encourage the greater consumption of beer. In those halcyon days, a nickel glass of beer assured the impecunious of as much food as he could tuck away in preparation for the next 24 hours.

Today's canape tray is entirely different—due to rising costs, increased knowledge of calories, and so on. It may be no more than a well-ripened Camembert, a tin of smoked mussels or pate de foie gras with salty crackers—or there may be a special titbit. There are three points to remember:

First: No more than two drinks should ever be served before dinner . . . and food (in the form of canapes, titbits or *bouchees*) should accompany the liquor. *This is an absolute and positive rule among true gastronomes and it must not be broken!* For one thing, there is little point in creating a gorgeous dinner for a group who have drunk too much to appreciate it.

Second: No matter how simple or few the components, a cocktail tray must *look* inviting . . . and black olives, crisp carrot sticks or bright radishes will fill innumerable chinks.

Third: The service of a special cocktail titbit may often gain an extra 15 minutes for the harassed chef to create the dinner masterpiece!

GUACAMOLE

A traditional south-of-the-border cocktail dip, to serve with sturdy potato chips or crisp crackers.

2 peeled ripe avocados	½ tsp black pepper
1 small white onion, grated	juice of half a lemon
1 tsp salt	

Mash the avocados through a sieve, add other ingredients, mix very smoothly and serve in a bowl lined with a few lettuce leaves. Dust the top with paprika.

NOTES: Avocados quickly blacken with air; guacamole should never be made more than half an hour in advance—in which case, cover the bowl with Saran wrap and keep in the refrigerator until the final moment.

Guacamole variations: add 2 crumbled crisp-cooked cold bacon slices—or 2 tablespoons of ground nuts (almonds, cashews, peanuts)—or a tablespoon of chili sauce—or a tablespoon of grated raw carrot—or a tablespoon of sherry and 6 minced black olives. . . .

STUFFED EGGS (2-Step Cookery)

Anyone can make deviled eggs, but a gourmet cook is not content with the dull mustard-cayenne variety. Stuffed eggs are best prepared in advance and allowed to chill gently for a minimum of two hours before serving.

For a very special cocktail hour, provide two or even three different stuffings. All start with peeled, halved hardboiled eggs—place the yolks in a bowl and mash:

1. 6 mashed hardboiled egg yolks, 1 T curry, 1 T mayonnaise, 1 tsp prepared mustard, 4 T fish or chicken paste. Garnish with drained capers.

2. 6 egg yolks mashed, 2 T whipped cream cheese, ¼ tsp anchovy paste, 1 T mayonnaise. (This should be a stiffer paste.)
   Garnish with a dusting of cinnamon.

3. 6 egg yolks mashed, 1 tsp chili sauce and 2 T flaked crabmeat, shrimp or lobstermeat . . . place in the

empty egg whites, and mask with the following mixture: 2 T mayonnaise, combined with 1 tsp curry powder. Garnish with an anchovy fillet.

4. 6 egg yolks mashed, 6 minced black olives, 2 T Roquefort or Bleu cheese. Mash thoroughly, and thin with a few drops of milk if necessary.
Garnish with toasted slivers of almonds, or pistachio nuts.

5. 6 egg yolks mashed, 2 T liver paste (or 2 mashed cooked chicken livers), 1 tsp curry powder, 1 T mayonnaise, salt and pepper.
Garnish with fresh parsley.

6. 6 egg yolks mashed, 3 T pate de foie gras, 1 tsp each of chervil, parsley and chives, salt and pepper.
Garnish with a black olive.

ANGELS ON HORSEBACK

8 oysters   salt, pepper, paprika
8 thin slices of bacon

Sprinkle oysters with salt, pepper and paprika. Wrap each oyster in a thin slice of bacon and secure with a toothpick. Broil until bacon is crisp, turning once to brown evenly. Serve hot.

PARMESAN CUBES

Bread cut in 1-inch cubes   1 cup grated Parmesan
   (day-old French bread or   ½ pound melted butter
   Italian)

Dunk the bread cubes in the butter—briefly, or they will absorb too much!—roll in grated Parmesan, and bake in the oven until golden brown—about 5 to 10 minutes in a very hot oven.

ROLLED CHEESE TOAST

8 slices very fresh white bread, crusts removed	Butter Soft Cheddar spread

Butter the bread, spread with cheese; roll up the slices—easily done by placing the bread buttered-side up on a damp kitchen towel. Fasten the rolls either with extra butter or by a toothpick; place in a shallow pan beneath the broiler flame and toast evenly on all sides . . . about 5 minutes over all.

PATE MAISON (2-Step Cookery)

A traditional molded chicken liver paste, to be used either as a cocktail spread with salted crackers or served in a small wedge as part of an hors d'oeuvres plate.

1 pound chicken livers	¼ tsp nutmeg
1 white onion	1½ tsp dry mustard
¾ cup rendered chicken fat (or melted butter)	⅛ tsp anchovy paste
	4 T grated white onion
1 tsp salt	1 T cognac brandy
⅓ tsp mace	

Step 1:

Wash livers, trim away any discolorations, place in a saucepan, add the whole peeled onion, barely cover with cold water and bring to a boil. Cover, reduce heat and simmer 20 minutes. Drain and discard the onion.

Grind the livers very *very* finely, using the finest blade of the grinder and putting them through a second time if necessary to reduce them to a smooth paste.

Add all the other ingredients, mixing very thoroughly. Pack in a straight-sided mold, cover with waxed paper, and chill overnight.

Step 2:

Unmold on a plate and slice thinly, for hors d'oeuvres—or serve in a ring of crisp salted crackers, for cocktail hour.

APPETIZERS

Classic first courses for a gourmet dinner are:

Hors d'Oeuvres (French)   Smorgasbord (Swedish)
Antipasto (Italian)

There are small but important differences between these, traditionally . . . and tradition is important in gourmet cookery,

Smorgasbord is an array of innumerable dishes, spread upon a separate buffet table, from which guests choose whatever they fancy and serve themselves on a salad-sized plate. It is served either as a first course, to be followed by meat-salad-dessert, or may be used as the main meal—in which case, guests are expected to return to the Smorgasbord table for second and third helpings, if they wish, and the meal is complete with dessert and coffee.

A true Smorgasbord offers a huge bowl of cold boiled shrimps, a whole turkey, and a large cold roast of beef, plus cole slaw, cucumber salad, potato salad, and a variety of molded fruit gelatines, flanked by dishes of cold salmon, herring fillets, tuna fish, all the usual garnishes of olives, pickles, carrot sticks, etc. There are usually also hot dishes of tiny boiled potatoes, meat balls, tiny frankfurters and baked beans.

A real Smorgasbord provides enough food for a small army! It is impossible to scale down a Smorgasbord for four—or even eight—people, but it can be presented to great advantage for the large buffet party.

Antipasto is prepared on individual plates in the kitchen, and served with a cruet of red wine vinegar and olive oil.

Hors d'Oeuvres, like the French who originated them, may go either way: served ready-prepared in the kitchen on individual plates, or in a series of dishes on rolling tea cart or Lazy Susan, from which seated guests select what they fancy.

The major difference between antipasto and hors d'oeuvres is that the latter are ready-mixed in their correct sauces, while Italian appetizers are plain and to be sprinkled at table with oil and vinegar. Salad-sized plates are used in all cases.

TRADITIONAL ANTIPASTO (for each serving)

half a hardboiled egg
1 slice of salami
2 or 3 drained sardines
¼ tin of tuna fish, drained and sprinkled with lemon juice
a cooked cold vegetable: asparagus tips, green beans, beets

Tomato slice
Celery stalk
Radishes, green and black olives, Greek olives
Pimiento section, crisscrossed with 2 anchovy fillets
Lentils, or chickpeas (Garbanzos beans)—1 T drained

Arrange the components attractively, starting with a tablespoon of lentils in the center, covered with pimiento and anchovy fillets, and surrounded by sardines next to salami, and tuna fish next to tomato slice, with the egg, celery, and garnishes used for color accents, and so on.

HORS D'OEUVRES

Includes many of the same ingredients used in Antipasto, but each is varied by the sauce. A traditional hors d'oeuvres includes:

Hardboiled egg, masked with mayonnaise and decorated with drained capers
Celery stalk and scallion, radishes, olives
A small slice of Pate Maison
Sardines and tuna fish, but put a dab of mayonnaise on the tuna fish and decorate with a strip of pimiento
Tomato slices
Haricots Blancs (white bean salad)
Vegetable Salads—any plain-cooked chilled vegetable, coated with Vinaigrette dressing
Celeri Remoulade

Artichoke Hearts
Anchovy fillets

The essential dressings for an hors d'oeuvres are mayonnaise; and Vinaigrette, which is also the true French dressing used for salads. (See Chapter 12.)

For last minute preparation of hors d'oeuvres vegetables, a basic Vinaigrette is 1 tablespoon of vinegar to 3 tablespoons of good olive oil, plus salt and pepper to taste, and these may be sprinkled directly into a mixing bowl after which the gentle mixing and turning will suffice to combine the dressing.

HARICOTS BLANCS (2-Step Cookery because it needs overnight chilling)

A white bean salad, usually pea or Navy beans, but a quick substitute is chickpeas (also called Garbanzos beans).

1 can chickpeas, drained
2 white onions, peeled and very thinly sliced

½ cup Vinaigrette dressing
¼ cup finely minced fresh parsley

Place a layer of chickpeas in a dish, cover with some of the sliced onions and parsley, and repeat until all ingredients are used. Pour Vinaigrette dressing over the dish, and mix very thoroughly. Chill overnight in the refrigerator.

LENTIL SALAD

1 can drained *chilled* lentils   ¼ cup Vinaigrette dressing

Combine and mix thoroughly; serve 2 small tablespoons for each hors d'oeuvres plate.

VEGETABLE SALADES

All true hors d'oeuvres present one or more *vegetable salades*—which are simply a thrifty French way to use up leftovers!

22

Suitable vegetables are: cauliflower, asparagus tips, French-style green beans, beets, carrots, a mixture of peas-limas-corn, artichoke hearts.

All *vegetable salades* are simply cold cooked vegetables coated with Vinaigrette dressing . . . and for home presentation, there is nothing wrong with placing different single-portion leftovers on each plate.

Vegetable salades are equally good in a Remoulade Sauce (see below): 2 cups mixed cold leftover vegetables, to ¼ cup Remoulade mixed with 1 T Vinaigrette dressing.

CELERI REMOULADE (2-Step Cookery)

Celeriac, marinated in French dressing, and served with a mustard-mayonnaise, either by itself or as part of a typical French hors d'oeuvres plate.

1. Peel a celery knob and cut in julienne strips. Cover with plain French dressing (1 tablespoon of vinegar to 3 tablespoons of olive oil, plus salt and pepper). Mix thoroughly to coat every piece of the celeriac with dressing; cover tightly and chill overnight.

2. Drain off the marinade, and replace with Remoulade Sauce, mixing well until celery is completely coated.

REMOULADE SAUCE

2 cups mayonnaise	1 T prepared mustard
½ cup sweet gherkins	1 T each minced parsley, tarragon, chervil
3 T drained capers	

Drain gherkins and capers; chop together finely and drain away any liquid. Combine all other ingredients and mix smoothly.

Variation:

Substitute 3 anchovy fillets for gherkins and a small tin of tomato paste for mustard. Substitute minced green pepper for 1 tablespoon of capers.

23

CELERIAC CHARPENTIER (2-Step Cookery)

1 celery root, scraped and cut in julienne strips	½ tsp pepper
	2 T tarragon vinegar
1 tsp salt	

Mix, cover tightly, and chill overnight.

Sauce:

2 T heavy cream	1 tsp meat stock (Bovril, Kitchen Bouquet)
1 tsp dry mustard	
1 egg yolk	½ tsp salt
1 T olive oil	¼ tsp pepper
1 tsp Worcestershire Sauce	1 pony of brandy (¾ ounce)

Mix the sauce thoroughly. Drain the celeriac and add to the sauce, turning gently to coat each sliver.

To serve: place a lettuce leaf on each plate, top with a slice of ripe tomato, and cover with the celeriac. Dust with paprika.

SPECIAL APPETIZERS

Aside from hors d'oeuvres and antipasto the shrimp cocktail is probably best known . . . and fresh crabmeat or lobster is interchangeable with shrimps.

FISH COCKTAIL SAUCE #1—bland

¼ cup mayonnaise	½ tsp sugar
½ cup chili sauce	½ tsp Worcestershire Sauce
1 T each: horseradish, lemon juice, grated onion	

Mix thoroughly, cover and chill before using.

FISH COCKTAIL SAUCE #2—sharp

½ cup catsup
¼ cup chili sauce
1 T lemon juice
1 tsp horseradish
1 tsp chopped parsley

1 T chopped green pepper
1 T chopped scallions
¼ tsp celery seed
2 T dry sherry

Mix thoroughly, chill before using.

HOT SHRIMPS

½ pound raw cleaned shrimps
   (or a thawed frozen package)
¼ cup butter
4 large fresh mushrooms,
   coarsely chopped

1 cup sour cream
1 tsp soy sauce
½ tsp salt
⅛ tsp Nepal pepper (or ¼
   tsp black pepper)
1 tsp paprika

Saute shrimps in butter for 4 minutes, add mushrooms and cook 10 minutes over gentle heat.

Separately combine sour cream and seasonings, color with the paprika and heat.

Combine shrimps and sauce, cook gently for 10 minutes or until thick and velvety.

Spoon the mixture into 4 buttered ramekins or large scallop shells, dust with grated Parmesan, and brown for a minute under broiler flame.

FRUITS DE MER

A thin pancake, rolled around creamed seafood, topped with Parmesan cheese, lightly broiled before serving.

These are not too difficult to prepare—and sometimes a double portion might take the place of an entree.

25

1 cooked lobster tail, or a small tin of lobster meat

½ cup fresh crabmeat, or a cleaned medium-sized tin

6 cooked shrimps, coarsely cut

6 scallops, coarsely cut

4 Cherrystone clams

4 oysters

4 mushrooms, chopped

1 cup mushroom soup, condensed

¼ cup Madeira, Marsala or dry sherry

1 tsp lemon juice

½ tsp paprika

1 tsp chopped chives

1 T minced parsley

1 T butter

1 T cream

salt, fresh pepper, grated Parmesan cheese

4 thin pancakes or 4 large scallop shells

Fruits de mer literally means "fruits of the sea." While it is usually served in a *crepe* (thin French pancake), it may also appear in scallop shells, buttered ramekins, or simply atop a buttered toast triangle.

Heat oven to 500.

Combine fish and shellfish with condensed mushroom soup, chopped fresh mushrooms, cream and wine, stir constantly and bring to high heat, then place over boiling water in a double boiler. Simmer gently while you prepare pancakes from any packaged mix. The pancakes should be very thin, cooked individually in butter, in a small skillet. Set them aside to keep warm.

Add all other ingredients (seasonings) to fish mixture and continue simmering for 5 minutes, while you butter a long shallow baking dish.

Place the pancakes one at a time: that is, place one at the end of the dish, spoon some of the creamed mixture into the center and fold over both pancake edges to cover the filling. Place the next pancake beside the first, etc. until all four *crepes* have been filled and are neatly distributed along the baking dish.

Cover with the remaining sauce, sprinkle generously with grated Parmesan cheese, and broil for 3 minutes or until tops are golden brown.

VEGETABLES A LA GRECQUE (2-Step Cookery)

A marinade in which to cook vegetables for appetizers or hors d'oeuvres. Greek cuisine uses even more olive oil than Italian . . .

2 cups water	1 bay leaf
½ cup olive oil	1 stalk of celery
¼ cup lemon juice, or white wine vinegar	1 tsp minced parsley

Combine in a saucepan, add a package of almost any frozen vegetable (or 1½ cups suitable raw vegetable) and cook gently for 15 minutes. Chill the vegetable *in* the cooking liquor overnight before serving.

Suitable vegetables: artichoke hearts, French-style beans, tiny Brussels sprouts, cauliflower, celery root, mixed vegetables.

HORS D'OEUVRE MUSHROOMS

1 pound tiny button mushrooms	6 T French (Vinaigrette) dressing
5 T olive oil	3 peeled sliced cold boiled potatoes
2 T butter	
4 minced shallots	2 large chopped peeled ripe tomatoes
1 clove garlic, pressed	
1 T minced parsley	4 lettuce leaves

Place lettuce leaves on 4 plates, top with chopped tomatoes surrounded by sliced potatoes.

Saute the whole tiny mushrooms in olive oil for 5 minutes. Add butter.

Mix shallots, garlic and parsley and sprinkle over mushrooms. Cook 1 minute, remove from fire, and thoroughly stir in the Vinaigrette dressing.

Pour the hot mushroom mixture over the tomatoes and potatoes.

CHAPTER 3

SOUP OF THE EVENING

Few people, it seems, eat soup any longer. In our diet conscious lives, many diners save their calorie-allowance for the main dish—but a clever gourmet chef never overlooks the possibilities in soup.

Of all the packaged foods available today, soup is probably the easiest to trick up into a replica of grandmother's stockpot. Almost anything can be used for soup—and almost any of these things is available either in tins or powders.

Hot soups replace an appetizer on a cold night; chilled soups, flanked by a chef's salad, are just right on a warm evening. Hearty soups, full of meat and vegetables and accompanied by plenty of garlic bread, are superb for Sunday nights, and for the lucky people within reach of a country garden, fresh vegetable soups are memorable for a quick supper after a day at the beach.

1. For richness of taste in cream soups, use milk in place of water—or cream in place of milk—in the amounts directed.

2. An authentic *petite marmite* takes time—but onion soup makes a good substitute.

3. Fresh vegetable soups require only cream and milk, plenty of butter, and almost any lightly cooked fresh vegetable . . .

4. For emergencies, combine two cans of almost any conceivable condensed soup, dilute with milk or water-and-wine, and create a satisfying dish.

For a fancy effect, hot soup should be served from a tureen at table—and the buffet dishes warmed by a candle are so impressive that people who thought they didn't like soup will eat two plates full!

FRESH VEGETABLE SOUPS

In any section of our country, according to season, there
will be local fresh vegetables—and all will make delicious
gourmet soups very simply. For instance . . .

FRESH CREAM OF TOMATO.

-8 sun-ripened tomatoes, peeled and quartered	4 tsp sugar
finely minced white onions	2 cups milk
T butter	salt, pepper, butter, fresh minced parsley
cup heavy cream	

Saute onions in butter until soft but not brown, add toma-
oes and simmer 15 minutes. Add sugar, salt, pepper, and
milk, and simmer for 10 minutes.

Prepare soup bowls with a teaspoon of butter and 2 table-
poons of cream in each. Pour hot soup into bowls, and
garnish with minced parsley.

The same general process works equally well with almost
ny local sun-ripened vegetables: fresh green peas, asparagus
ips, tiny Brussels sprouts, little carrots or lima beans, fresh
orn kernels or tiny string beans. . . .

SQUASH SOUP

package frozen squash (or 2 slices peeled pumpkin, steamed soft and pureed)	1 grated white onion
	½ cup vermicelli (optional)
cups milk	2 T butter
cups heavy cream	salt, pepper, minced parsley

Place squash, milk, cream and onion in the top of a double
boiler, and simmer for 25 minutes, stirring to mix occasionally.

Meanwhile boil the vermicelli for 15 minutes in water to
cover. When tender, drain thoroughly and add to the squash
puree, together with 2 T butter, season to taste with a little
salt and pepper, and serve with a garnish of minced parsley.

MUSHROOM SOUP

1 pound fresh mushrooms, sliced thinly
2 cups milk
3 shallots, minced
2 T butter
1 cup heavy cream
4 egg yolks
½ cup sweet sherry
salt, pepper, and butter

Marinate the mushrooms in the milk, while you saute the shallots in butter (for 5 minutes). Combine in a deep sauce pot, add the cream, salt and pepper to taste, and hold it at a slow boil for 25 minutes.

Prepare 4 soup bowls with an egg yolk and 2 tablespoon of sherry in each. Pour the hot soup into each bowl, stirring rapidly to distribute the egg yolk and sherry into the soup. Garnish with fresh minced parsley if you wish.

OYSTER STEW

4 minced shallots (or scallions)
4 T butter
1½ dozen oysters with their liquor (or 2 tins drained oysters)
2 cups milk
2 cups heavy cream
pepper, salt
2 glasses dry sherry
4 teaspoons butter

Simmer shallots in 4 tablespoons of butter for 5 minutes, add oysters and liquor. Bring to a boil, add milk and cream, salt and pepper. Simmer 2 minutes, add sherry, and again bring to the boil.

Place a teaspoon of butter in each serving bowl, pour soup over, and serve with Parmesan cheese toast.

PEA SOUP

2 packages frozen peas
1 large minced onion
1 cup milk
1 cup heavy cream
4 T butter
2 tsp cornstarch, dissolved in 2 T milk

30

Boil the peas and onion together until soft; drain and puree. Add milk, cream and butter, place in a double boiler and let come to a boil. Thicken with the cornstarch mixture, and cook gently for 5 minutes, stirring smoothly. Season with salt, pepper and paprika to taste.

CRAB SPECIALITÉ

A very special richly delicious soup, to be followed by a chef's salad, fresh fruit and coffee.

½ pound fresh crab meat—or 1 can cleaned Geisha crab meat
½ cup dry sherry
½ can condensed pea soup
½ can condensed tomato soup
1 cup heavy cream

Mix the crabmeat with sherry and let it stand. Combine soups and cream and bring to a boil very slowly.

Reduce heat sharply, add the crabmeat and sherry, and simmer for 10 minutes, adding a little extra milk or cream if the soup is too thick.

Serve in soup bowls with a tablespoon of dry sherry added to each.

AVGOLEMONO

A Greek chicken-lemon soup, extremely simple to make.

5 cups chicken bouillon (dissolve soup packets in 5 cups of water, or use tinned consomme)
¼ cup plain rice
2 eggs
juice of a lemon
seasonings (salt, pepper, paprika)

Bring the bouillon to a boil, add rice and simmer 20 minutes. Meanwhile, beat eggs with lemon juice; add ¼ cup of the hot bouillon and blend, stirring constantly.

Remove the soup pot from heat and combine with egg-lemon mixture, season with salt, pepper and paprika, and serve very hot.

This soup may be kept hot for a few minutes, but should *never* be allowed to boil again after the egg mixture has been added.

SOUR CREAM SOUP—*A typically Russian dish*

6 cups chicken stock (or 6 packs MBT Chicken Consomme powder dissolved in 6 cups hot water)
1 teaspoon cumin seed
3 boiled potatoes, peeled and diced

1 cup sour cream
1 cup sweet heavy cream
1 T flour
salt, pepper

Combine stock, seasonings and cumin seed in a saucepan, bring to the boil and simmer 10 minutes. Make a smooth paste of the flour and sour cream; pour a cup of hot stock onto it, beating until smooth, and add this mixture to the pot of stock. Stir thoroughly, add the sweet cream and potatoes, and simmer 10 minutes over very low heat. Do not allow the soup to boil after adding the sweet cream. Serve hot.

BEER SOUP

This is a hearty soup from Middle Europe, to be served with pumpernickel.

1 quart beer
1 quart water
1 cup heavy cream

1 tablespoon butter
2 tablespoons sugar
3 egg yolks

Combine beer and water, bring to a boil, and add sugar and butter. Simmer for 25 minutes. Beat egg yolks thoroughly; add cream and beat again very thoroughly. Finally add a little of the hot beer to cream and egg mixture—very slowly, stirring constantly to prevent curdling. Return the mixture to the saucepan, and heat for 5 minutes, but do not allow the soup to boil.

SNOWPEA SOUP

1 pound of snowpeas (or *very* young fresh peas in pods)
1 small Boston lettuce
2 small white onions
1 handful of fresh spinach (about a cup)

1 T flour
2 T butter
2 cups boiling water
2 cups thin cream
salt, pepper, sugar
1 sprig of fresh mint (½ tsp dried mint)

Coarsely chop all the vegetables and fresh mint—use peas without shelling.

Melt butter, add vegetables and stir occasionally for about 5 minutes over low heat. Sprinkle flour over vegetables and stir gently until all is absorbed and smooth.

Add boiling water very gradually, stirring constantly to prevent flour lumps. Add the milk, stir smooth, and season to taste with salt, pepper, and a generous pinch of sugar.

Simmer 20 minutes, strain into soup cups, and top with a dusting of paprika.

AVOCADO SOUP

½ dried chili pepper
3 large avocados
2 cups chicken consomme

1 cup heavy cream
½ teaspoon pepper
1 teaspoon salt

Mix the crumbled chili pepper with the meat of 2 avocados, and crush to a pulp with a potato masher. Force this mixture through a sieve into the top of a double boiler, and add the chicken broth (either a can of consomme or dissolved packets of MBT). Heat over direct heat until the soup boils, then place over hot water; add the cream, mix thoroughly, cover and again heat to boiling point. Skin and seed the third avocado and cut into small chunks. At the last moment before serving, add these chunks to the soup, plus salt and pepper.

CLAM BROTH

12 Cherrystone clams	2 tablespoons fresh chopped
3 shallots	parsley
2 cups water	1 cup heavy whipped cream
1 tablespoon olive oil	

Place scrubbed clams in a deep sauce pot, sprinkle with olive oil, add water, parsley and minced shallots. Steam the clams open over a medium flame (10-15 minutes), while whipping the cream. Then strain the clam broth into 4 cups, add three shelled clams to each serving, top with a generous tablespoon of the whipped cream, dusted with paprika.

COLD SOUPS are for warm evenings, to be followed by an omelet, salad, fresh fruit and coffee.

All cold soups are two-step cookery, of course, since they require time to chill.

GAZPACHO

There are many methods of making this famous Spanish cold cucumber soup; all are good.

Gazpacho de Malaga

4 cups chicken consomme (soup packets dissolved in water)	1 cucumber, peeled and seeded
2 cloves of garlic, pressed	½ sweet red pepper, seeds removed
1 small white onion, grated	4 T cooked rice
1 large ripe tomato, peeled and seeds removed	2 T olive oil

Dice tomato, cucumber and red pepper; combine all the ingredients, mix thoroughly and chill overnight.

Gazpacho de Cordoba

2 peeled seeded cucumbers, finely cubed
2 cloves pressed garlic
2 T olive oil
2 cups water
2 cups heavy cream
2 tsp cornstarch
1 tsp salt

Mix garlic, cucumbers and olive oil; let stand.

Bring water to a boil, add salt, and cornstarch mixed to a smooth paste with 3 tablespoons of cold water. Stir until thick and smooth.

Pour cornstarch mixture over cucumbers. Cool, and slowly add the cream, stirring constantly. Chill overnight and serve ice-cold.

TARATA

A Levantine version of Gazpacho, substituting eggplant for the cucumbers.

2 green peppers, skinned and seeded
2 small eggplants, skinned and seeded
6 T olive oil
3 cups yoghurt
1 tsp salt
½ tsp pepper
2 cloves of garlic, pressed
a pinch each of Cayenne and powdered mint

Cooked minced peppers and eggplants in oil very gently for about 15 minutes; do not brown. When soft, mash finely, and mix with all other ingredients. Chill overnight and serve ice-cold.

COLD FRUIT SOUP—*typically Scandinavian*

1 medium-sized tin each: prunes, apricots, pears
3 tart apples, peeled, cored and chopped
1 cinnamon stick
2 T cornstarch, mixed to a paste with a little cold water

35

Combine fruits (with their juices), apple and cinnamon, and add 1 cup water. Simmer very gently until the fruit is extremely mushy (about 10 minutes). Force through a sieve into a saucepan, add the cornstarch mixed with water, bring to a boil and stir smoothly, cooking for 2 minutes. Cool overnight before serving.

NOTE: Almost any fruit can be used for the cold Scandinavian fruit soups: cherries, strawberries, raspberries—even peaches or nectarines . . . but the basic theory is always the same: Reduce the fruit to a mush with enough water to aid in extracting the natural juice; sweeten to taste (if you are using fresh fruit); spice with a cinnamon stick or 1 teaspoon ground nutmeg; thicken with cornstarch and water. Chill overnight, and serve with a few bits of fresh fruit.

ICED SHRIMP SOUP

1 pound cooked shrimp	½ cup heavy cream
3 cups water	1 teaspoon fresh minced chives
3 tablespoons bread crumbs	
1 tablespoon grated lemon rind	2 teaspoons fresh minced parsley
1 cup white wine	½ cup cucumber
1 egg yolk	salt and pepper

Reserve 8 shrimp for garnishing; grind the remainder or pound in a mortar. Combine ground shrimps with water, wine, bread crumbs, lemon rind, and *generous* pinch of ground nutmeg in a saucepan. Bring to a boil, and cook for 7 minutes, stirring constantly. Strain through a fine sieve and return to low heat.

Beat together the egg yolk and cream and add, stirring gently. Heat until shrimp soup thickens slightly but do not allow to boil. Finally, remove from fire; cool, add the chives, parsley and peeled diced cucumber. Chill overnight in the refrigerator, and serve with a garnish of the remaining shrimps, coarse-chopped, plus a large tablespoon of sour cream or yoghurt.

CHAPTER 4

ONE MAN'S *POISSON* . . .

If you think you do not like fish, you will never qualify as a gourmet. Gourmets eat and *enjoy* everything—when properly prepared. Your dislike may come from the way in which fish is cooked. Try it baked or broiled—both of which minimize cooking odors.

Fish is low in calories, thus good for diets. It is also extremely versatile in presentation . . . for instance:

1. *Any* fish fillet can be broiled, baked or sauteed in plenty of butter.

2. *Any* fish fillet can be spread with a bit of anchovy paste —or rolled about chopped shrimps, oysters or clams before baking.

3. *Any* fish fillet can be baked in a sauce of melted butter, white wine, parsley, chives, chervil, tarragon, onion, minced scallions or shallots, with a few tablespoons of lemon juice and some slivered blanched nuts.

4. *Any* creamed fish will respond to a dash of nutmeg in the sauce.

5. *Any* creamed fish will taste richer with a few tablespoons of white wine added to the sauce. If you add sherry, the creamed fish automatically becomes *"a la Newburg"*— and what's wrong with that?

6. Adding ¼ cup of mixed pickling spice to the water in which you prepare any fish or shellfish will make a considerable difference in flavor!

CLAMS CASINO, OYSTERS ROCKEFELLER, COQUILLES ST. JACQUES

Three traditional recipes, capable of many variations, which are basically the same: shellfish, combined with a simple sauce, replaced in the shell and baked until bubbly.

37

CLAMS CASINO

Allow 8 to 12 Cherrystones per portion for a main dish; clams for each appetizer service. Have the clams opened a the fish market and packed on the half-shells.

Sauce:

¼ cup butter
1 tsp anchovy paste
¼ cup minced green pepper
¼ cup grated onion

2 tsp fine-chopped pimient
4 slices raw bacon, cut i
   tiny pieces
salt, pepper, lemon juice

Heat the oven to 450.

Remove clams from shells and discard the juice. Bed the shells firmly in a baking pan, surrounded by crumpled aluminum foil to keep them upright (rock salt is fancier, if you have it).

Cream butter and anchovy paste, distribute evenly among the shells. Insert a clam in each shell and sprinkle with lemon juice.

Combine chopped pepper, pimiento, onion, salt and pepper, and distribute among the clam shells. Top with bacon bits, and bake until top browns: about 20 minutes.

OYSTERS ROCKEFELLER

Oysters, highly seasoned, baked on a bed of spinach.

3 dozen oysters, opened on the half-shell at the fish market
1 package cooked frozen chopped spinach
2 cups white sauce, made from condensed cream soup (celery)
3 T sherry
1 egg

2 T butter
1 T each minced onion and parsley
½ tsp Worcestershire Sauce
¼ tsp salt
½ tsp Monosodium Glutamate (Accent Powder)
6 drops Tabasco
a dash of nutmeg, and of Nepal pepper

Heat the oven to 375.

Bed oysters in their shells upright in crumpled aluminum foil in a baking pan. Sprinkle lightly with sherry.

Cook spinach till slightly underdone, and drain thoroughly.

Meanwhile, combine condensed soup with ½ cup milk and heat gently. Add a beaten egg, blend thoroughly and place over hot water.

In a separate skillet, melt the butter and saute onion for 3 minutes. Add drained spinach and ¼ cup of the soup, plus all seasonings, and blend. Saute for 3 minutes, distribute over the waiting oysters. Top with the rest of the soup-sauce, sprinkle with grated Parmesan cheese and bake for 15 minutes until light brown.

COQUILLES ST. JACQUES

Scallops in a wine sauce, baked in their shells. Any shellfish will respond to this treatment, alone or in combination.

Large scallop and clam shells can be bought in any gourmet shop; once you have them, never let them go.

1½ cups white wine	½ pound mushrooms
1 bay leaf	6 shallots or a small white onion
2 T fresh chopped parsley	
¼ tsp each thyme and fennel seeds	1 T butter
1½ pounds scallops	1 tsp lemon juice

Alternate Sauce Preparation:

#1	#2
1 tin condensed mushroom soup	4 T flour
2 egg yolks	2 egg yolks
4 T heavy cream	4 T heavy cream
	1 tsp salt
	4 T butter

Combine wine, bay leaf, parsley, thyme and fennel; bring to a boil, add scallops and simmer 10 minutes. Sea scallops should be cut in pieces, but the tiny Eastern bay scallops are used whole. Drain, but reserve the hot liquid.

Separately, saute sliced mushrooms, shallots or onion in butter and lemon juice, for 10 minutes. Strain and combine all the hot liquids in one pan, all the solids in another.

If you use *Alternate Sauce #1:* Start heating mushroom soup in a double boiler while scallops and mushrooms are cooking. Prepare the egg yolks, lightly beaten in a cup, and mixed with the cream.

Thin soup with 1½ cups of the hot liquids, stirring smoothly. Add a bit of this to the cream and egg yolks, blend smooth, and pour back into the sauce. Stir gently as it thickens, for about 5 to 10 minutes, and combine with scallops and mushrooms.

Alternate Sauce #2 (This is the traditional preparation method)

Melt butter in a saucepan, add flour and stir over low heat till free of lumps. Gradually thin with 2 full cups of the hot scallop-mushroom liquid, stirring constantly. Remove from the fire; combine egg yolks and cream, slightly beaten together; add a little sauce to egg yolks and stir smooth, then return to main sauce pot. Blend thoroughly, and combine with scallops and mushrooms.

Final operation, no matter which sauce you prepare: Distribute the creamed fish mixture among 4 large scallop shells, top with crumbs and grated Parmesan cheese, brown under a broiler for 5 minutes.

BOUILLABAISSE, CIOPPINO or ZUPPA DA PESCA, and PAELLA

These are traditional French, Italian and Spanish versions of the same dish: a fish soup-stew, which is served as a main dish accompanied by a green salad and plenty of crisp French or Italian-style bread.

Paella dates from the 14th Century, is supposed to have been created by a Spanish king who would obviously have been happier as a chef (just as Louis XVI of France ought to have been a carpenter). The name is a corruption of "Para Ella," because it was dedicated to the king's mistress-of-the moment. Paella combines chicken and sweet sausage with shellfish and rice. It will take every blessed minute of your quick-cookery allotment, plus plenty of preparation in advance—and perhaps it should not be included here, but it *definitely belongs* with Bouillabaisse and Cioppino.

Bouillabaisse depends primarily upon several kinds of fish, both firm and soft-fleshed, with a modest addition of lobster and clams. Literal translation of Bouillabaisse is "boil-stop" —and the secret of the dish lies in *fierce* boiling, exactly as directed. Another secret is the combination of fish; an authentic Bouillabaisse de Marseilles (where the dish was originated) uses at least *seven* different kinds of fish, and many of them are varieties unobtainable in our country. In making a bouillabaisse, however, remember that the flavors of several different kinds of fish must predominate; the shellfish are added merely as window-dressing.

Cioppino, or *Zuppa da Pesca*, is exactly opposite from Bouillabaisse. Here, you wish the flavors of shellfish to predominate, and the bits of softer fish are the window-dressing. The cooking method of Cioppino is slightly more leisurely than for Bouillabaisse, but a final period of *fierce* boiling will make the smooth mixture of oil and liquid for the soup.

PAELLA (2-Step Cookery)

1 dozen Cherrystone clams	½ cup chopped onions
1 box each: frozen peas and artichoke hearts	½ tsp each: tarragon, oregano, chervil, salt, paprika, chives
1 large tin canned tomatoes	
1 box cleaned frozen shrimp	½ tsp saffron (soaked in 1 T hot water)
2 small sweet Spanish or Italian sausages	
	¼ tsp pepper
Diced meat from one small chicken (pre-cooked)	2 cups consomme
	1 cup quick-cooking rice
½ cup olive oil	1 minced clove garlic

Step 1: steam the chicken (or cook in a pressure-cooker); cool slightly and dice the meat. Slightly undercook peas, artichoke hearts and shrimp.

Step 2: saute onions and garlic in olive oil. Add consomme rice, seasonings, chicken, tomatoes and sliced sausages. Cove and simmer 10 minutes, checking occasionally to stir an add extra consomme if needed.

Add peas, artichoke hearts, cooked shrimps, and plac well-scrubbed clams on top. Cover tightly and steam for 1 minutes or until the clam shells open. Serve with strips o pimiento for decoration.

Real Spaniards use: eels, lobster, crabs, fried eggplan sticks and oysters, mushrooms—any or all. Paella is one o the great dishes, to be made with whatever is available.

BOUILLABAISSE

2 pounds of mixed fish: cod or halibut, bass, mackerel, smelts, porgy or flounder, eel, red snapper, whiting, perch. . . . Have the fish cut in 1½ inch serving pieces, bones and all.

1 small cooked lobster, cut in serving pieces (shell & all)

1 dozen clams, well-scrubbed in their shells

¼ cup olive oil

3 sliced onions

3 crushed garlic cloves

2 sliced celery stalks (including the leaves)

2 chopped scallions or 1 peeled chopped leek

2 crumbled bay leaves

4 peeled chopped very-ripe tomatoes (or a drained large tin)

4 cups bouillon

1 tsp salt

½ tsp pepper

¼ tsp nutmeg

½ tsp saffron, steeped in 1 T hot water

½ tsp grated orange peel

2 cups white wine

2 tsp chopped parsley

OPTIONAL—if you live near the seashore:

2 small boiled crabs
Mussels, in place of clams

2 dozen cleaned, deveined raw shrimp

Place vegetables and seasonings in a large pot—choose one with a tight cover!

Distribute the firm-fleshed fish (cod, halibut, eel, turbot, snapper, mackerel, sea bass) atop the vegetables, add olive oil, wine, and a cup of hot water.

Bring to the boil, and boil VIOLENTLY for 5 minutes.

Add the soft-fleshed fish (smelts, whiting, porgy, perch, etc.) and boil violently for exactly 3 minutes.

Add the cooked cut lobster and scrubbed clams (as well as crabs, mussels and shrimps, if you are using them) and again boil fiercely for 8 minutes.

Remove *at once* from the fire.

To serve Bouillabaisse, use the large old-fashioned soup *dishes* if you are lucky enough to have them. Garlic or Parmesan toasted stale bread—plus a substantial green salad—go with Bouillabaisse. Put a piece of stale bread in the bottom of the soup plate, apportion the various kinds of fish and shellfish on top, and add enough of the liquid to float the fish. Serve plenty of extra bread for sopping up the juice.

CIOPPINO (or Zuppa da Pesca)

1 pound bass, cut in serving slices

1 large chopped onion

2 cooked lobsters, cut in pieces (shell and all)

2 minced cloves of garlic

2 T minced parsley

1 cooked crab (cut in pieces like the lobster)

1 large chopped green pepper (seeds removed)

1 package frozen cleaned shrimp

1 bay leaf

2 cloves

12 scrubbed Little Neck clams or mussels

1 large tin drained tomatoes

1 cup red wine

½ cup chopped mushrooms

1 cup hot water

½ cup olive oil

1 tsp salt

1 dash Cayenne pepper

Saute: onions, garlic, parsley, green pepper and seasonings in warm olive oil for 5 minutes. Add mushrooms, tomatoes, bass and shrimp, water and wine. Cover tightly and cook briskly for 10 minutes. Add lobsters, crab and clams or mussels; cover tightly and cook briskly for 10 minutes.

Serve in large soup plates, with plenty of fresh Italian bread, a glass of red wine, and a plain green salad.

43

SOLE MARGUERY

Fish fillets in creamy shellfish sauce.

This recipe will require all your charm at the fish market
—because you need so many ingredients and such small
quantities of each—but the result is worth cajolery.

4 fillets of sole
8 oysters
8 Cherrystone clams
1 cooked package cleaned
   shrimp (or 12 fresh-
   cooked, shelled)
4 sea scallops
1 cup Sauterne
1 cup water
½ lemon, sliced thin

1 tin condensed mushroom
   soup
¾ cup milk
2 T sherry
¼ tsp each dry mustard and
   paprika
½ tsp Worcestershire Sauce
4 mushroom caps
4 T minced parsley
Grated Parmesan cheese

Heat oven to 375.

Combine Sauterne, water and lemon, bring to a boil, lower
heat sharply and poach fish fillets for 3 minutes. Remove fish
to a buttered shallow baking dish. Surround with drained
shellfish and decorate with mushroom caps; arrange for easy
service in 4 portions. Combine soup, milk, sherry, mustard,
paprika, Worcestershire, and blend smoothly. Gently pour
over the fish fillets. Bake 15 minutes in the oven, and remove.
Increase heat to broil; dust the dish with cheese, parsley and
paprika, and broil for 4 minutes or until lightly browned.

LOBSTER THERMIDOR

Lobster, in a rich wine sauce, baked in the lobster shell.
A traditional dish, named for the French Revolution . . .
one cannot but applaud the single-mindedness that could
create a new recipe in the shadow of the Guillotine, but perhaps that is why the French remain the masters of gastronomy.

2 cooked lobsters, split in half at the fish market
1 tin condensed cream of mushroom soup
2 T white wine
½ cup thin cream
2 T butter

1 tsp grated onion
4 minced mushroom stems (optional)
Grated Parmesan cheese, bread crumbs, and 2 more tablespoons butter

Remove all meat from lobsters, including claw meat; reserve the cleaned body shells. Cut lobster meat into small pieces.

Melt 2 T butter, add onion, mushroom stems and lobster, and saute for 5 minutes.

Combine soup, wine and cream in a double boiler and heat until well blended and smooth, adding some minced parsley if you like. Add lobster mixture, and heat gently for 5 minutes. Then apportion among the lobster shells, sprinkle thickly with grated cheese and dust with bread crumbs. Dot with remaining butter and bake in a hot (450) oven for 10 minutes, or until the top browns.

WHITEBAIT

Crisp-fried little fish, eaten with French Fries and a good green salad . . . one of the few really good British dishes.

This is a real delicacy, not always available at the fish market—but if you happen to be near water, and *fresh* "shiners" can be had from the fishing bait store, you've got whitebait!

3 pounds of whitebait
Seasoned flour—1 cup or more, plus 1 tsp salt, ½ tsp pepper, 1 tsp minced chervil or fresh parsley, ½ tsp paprika

Heat the fish-frying deep fat kettle.

Rinse the whitebait (or shiners) thoroughly; drain any excess water, and toss them in a paper bag filled with the seasoned flour. Place the floured whitebait in a frying basket, immerse in hot fat for 2 minutes, drain, garnish with lemon and fresh parsley and serve with plenty of tartar sauce.

Whitebait should be crisp and well-drained, and it's acceptable to eat them in your fingers—holding each fish by its little tail and dunking in the tartar sauce.

HOMARD A L'ARMORICAINE

Lobster in a sauce of wine, tomatoes and onions.

4 or 5 lobster tails (about 4 pounds in their shells), defrosted and cut in two or three pieces each
¼ cup olive oil
¼ pound plus 2 T butter
1 crushed garlic clove
1 minced shallot or scallion
1 T tomato paste
3 large ripe tomatoes, peeled
2 cups dry white wine
3 T flour
½ cup Cognac
1 T minced parsley
1 tsp tarragon
1 small bay leaf, crumbled
¼ tsp thyme
salt, pepper, a dash of Cayenne, a dash of Tabasco
hot water (about 2 cups)

Heat oven to medium (375).

Heat olive oil and 3 T butter in a large sauce pan; when very hot, add the lobster pieces, plus salt and pepper. Saute the lobster for 5 minutes, turning and stirring over fairly high heat until cooked; drain away the fat.

Add garlic and minced shallot to the pan, plus Cognac; heat briefly and flame, turning and twisting the pan until all lobster pieces are bathed in the flaming brandy. When flames die, add the white wine, tomato paste, coarsely cut tomatoes, parsley, tarragon, bay leaf, thyme. Mix well and transfer to an ovenproof casserole . . . adding enough water to bring the sauce just to cover lobster. Stir gently to distribute water in and around the sauce.

Cover and bake for 20 minutes. Remove the lobster pieces to a warm serving dish.

Over high heat, bring the sauce to a boil and reduce for 5 minutes. Stir the flour smooth with a little water, crushing out all lumps. Add a bit of the hot sauce to the flour, and stir until there are no lumps; then return to the sauce pot and simmer very gently for 5 minutes, adding a dash of

Cayenne and a dash of Tabasco sauce. Pour the sauce over the lobster pieces, and sprinkle with parsley.

SHRIMP

To a gourmet, shrimp are ubiquitous and indispensable. Hot or cold, plain or sauced, shrimp are a universal American favorite—because we have such *good* shrimp—and via deep freezing, they are available everywhere in the country. But other countries also like shrimp; next to our own delicious Mexican Gulf shrimp, the best in the world are probably Korean.

A gourmet cook can do absolutely anything with shrimp! They go into sauces, either whole or sliced; they can be used in *any* traditional course but dessert . . . and since there exists a liver ice cream (for diabetic diets), perhaps shrimps could also be used this way!

Shrimp can be boiled in the shell: place in cold water with pickling spices, if you like; bring to the boil and cook no more than 4 minutes. Or shrimp can be shelled and deveined for use in special recipes . . . or they can be cut in fancy ways (particularly for Oriental dishes), with or without an inch of tail shell left behind for eating in the fingers. A Smorgasbord serves cold boiled shrimp unshelled; you do the work of skinning before you dunk in a sauce.

One way or another, shrimp are runner-up in indispensability to onions. No true gourmet can live without either of them.

SCAMPI, TEMPURA, DE JONGHE and
WEST INDIAN SHRIMPS

Italian, Japanese, East and West Indian shrimp treatments —just to give a sampling.

Scampi is the Italian word for shrimp. There are many ways to prepare them, but all are basically broiled shrimp with garlic and tomatoes. The real variation lies in whether or not they are shelled.

Most Scampi dishes are shelled raw shrimp with a bit of

tail shell remaining, but some of the finest Italian restaurants serve Scampi in the shell, merely cutting down the inside curve and spreading apart to form a butterfly-shape. The latter is attractive, but hard to eat; it can only be used with the very largest shrimps or prawns.

Basic Scampi

1½ pounds cleaned large raw shrimp (or 2 defrosted boxes)
½ cup olive oil
½ cup minced parsley
4 minced garlic cloves
2 minced shallots or scallions
¼ tsp oregano

Saute shrimp in olive oil for 5 minutes over high heat, shaking or stirring briskly until cooked. Season with salt and pepper and remove to a hot ovenproof platter, draining off the oil.

Add remaining ingredients to olive oil, saute over medium high flame for 3 minutes, shaking the pan briskly. Pour sauce over shrimp and broil for 2 minutes.

Scampi a la Casa

1½ pounds raw cleaned shrimp (or 2 defrosted cleaned boxes)
½ cup flour
½ cup olive oil
½ cup dry white wine
2 T brandy
2 tsp tomato paste
2 tsp lemon juice
¼ cup water
1 T minced fresh parsley
2 minced shallots or scallions
salt, pepper, a dash of Cayenne

Roll the washed shrimp in flour, brown thoroughly in hot olive oil and drain off the oil to a separate saucepan.

Add wine and brandy to shrimp, warm for a few seconds, then flame; stir shrimps briskly until flames die. Reduce heat and cook very gently until all liquid is absorbed by the shrimps.

Meanwhile, combine olive oil, tomato paste, salt, pepper, Cayenne and water, and blend for 5 minutes over low heat.

Finally, pour this sauce over shrimp, add parsley and

scallions, simmer for a final 5 minutes. Remove to serving plates, sprinkle with the lemon juice, and serve.

Tempura (Japanese)

Shrimp in a batter, deep-fried.

2 pounds raw shrimp, shelled, deveined—*but tails left onl*	½ tsp salt
	2 beaten eggs
	1 cup milk
1 cup flour	hot frying fat

Split each shrimp neatly down the back and spread open to form a butterfly-shape. Leave the tails on, so you can hold them to dip in the sauce.

Combine flour, salt, eggs and milk to make a thin batter, and do not fuss over small flour lumps. *The batter must be used at once.* Dip shrimp into batter, drain briefly, and fry in hot deep fat for 3 minutes.

Tempura are served hot, with side dishes of chutney, grated fresh horseradish or grated fresh ginger, as well as soy sauce.

Shrimp de Jonghe (East Indian)

Shrimp baked with herbs, spices and sherry.

2 pounds cleaned cooked shrimp (or 2 frozen boxes)	⅛ tsp each: nutmeg, mace, thyme
1 clove garlic	½ cup dry sherry
¼ tsp each: tarragon, parsley, chervil, white onion, shallot	½ tsp pepper
	1 tsp salt
½ cup sweet butter	Extra bread crumbs and ¼ cup melted butter
1 cup fine bread crumbs	

Heat oven to 450.

Cook frozen shrimp 15 minutes in boiling water, drain thoroughly. Mash garlic clove to a paste, add everything else but sherry, melted butter, and extra bread crumbs. Cream

49

the mixture until soft and smooth, then carefully thin with sherry.

Generously butter a casserole dish; make alternate layers of shrimps and the bread crumb mixture. Top with the extra bread crumbs and pour the melted butter over the dish.

Bake 15 minutes.

West Indian Shrimp

1½ pounds cooked cleaned shrimp (or 2 packages frozen)
2 T olive oil
1 T Angostura Bitters
1 tsp chervil

½ tsp marjoram (or oregano)
½ tsp thyme
½ tsp cumin (powdered)
¼ tsp saffron, soaked in 1 tablespoon warm water
Grated cheese

Place frozen cleaned shrimp in boiling water, bring again to the boil and simmer briskly for 15 minutes. Meanwhile heat your broiling oven.

Drain shrimp and saute quickly in olive oil. Sprinkle with the bitters during cooking.

Remove to a shallow casserole, and sprinkle the shrimps with the herbs and saffron. Top with a generous sprinkle of grated Parmesan, and broil until lightly browned (about 5 minutes).

Serve with steamed rice.

Shrimp a la Creme

A shrimp version of Coquille St. Jacques, using sour cream for the sauce.

1½ pounds deveined raw shelled shrimp
⅓ cup butter
½ pound fresh sliced mushrooms

1½ cups sour cream
1 tsp soy sauce
1 T paprika
salt, pepper, Parmesan cheese

Saute cleaned shrimp in butter for 3 minutes, add the mushrooms and saute for 8 minutes. Heat sour cream, soy and seasonings.

50

Combine shrimp and sauce, blend and cook about 4 minutes (until thick and smooth).

Transfer to scallop shells or a buttered casserole, sprinkle with grated Parmesan cheese and brown for 4 minutes under the broiler or until golden brown on top.

POMPANO

A Florida delicacy, baked with nuts and brandy. Consider this recipe for any combination of fresh fish fillets and suitable nuts.

2 pounds pompano, cut in 4 pieces	½ cup ground blanched hazelnuts
2 shallots, minced	1 pony of brandy
¼ lb butter	

Heat oven to 450.

Melt butter and saute shallots, while you place pompano sections in a buttered baking pan. Sprinkle generously with the hazelnuts, gently pour over melted butter and shallots.

Bake 20 minutes, basting every 5 minutes to prevent dryness. Add the brandy, and flame. Return to oven for 3 minutes, and serve with lemon wedges.

CRABMEAT CASSEROLE

Very rich shellfish casserole of crabmeat and lobster in a cream sauce.

½ pound fresh crab meat (or 2 cleaned tins)	1 T flour
	salt and pepper to taste
½ cup lobster meat (or ½ pound cleaned cooked shrimps)	2 T brandy (optional)
	2 slices crisp-cooked bacon
½ cup heavy cream	Grated Parmesan cheese and bread crumbs
¼ lb butter, melted	

Heat oven to 450.

Saute mushrooms in melted butter for 5 minutes, dusting

with flour and blending; add cream and stir until slightly thickened. Thin with the brandy, if you use it.

Cook bacon crisp in a separate pan, and drain from fat. Place crab meat, lobster or shrimps, in buttered casserole dish. Cover with the mushroom-cream sauce, and top with crumbled bacon bits. Dust with bread crumbs and sprinkle generously with grated cheese. Bake 10 minutes in the oven, brown 5 minutes under a broiler flame.

BAKED OYSTERS

2 dozen oysters, opened on the half-shell	2 T meat stock
	2 T chili sauce
1 clove garlic, pressed	4 mushrooms
1 T minced parsley	4 shallots
½ cup melted butter	2 T grated cheese
pepper, salt	2 T bread crumbs
2 tsp Worcestershire Sauce	

Combine parsley, garlic, pepper, salt, Worcestershire, meat stock and chili sauce with ¼ melted butter. Mix well. Dip each oyster into this sauce and replace in its shell on a baking pan. Distribute the additional sauce among the oysters.

Chop mushrooms and shallots finely, mix with cheese and crumbs and minced parsley. Sprinkle over each oyster, add the remaining melted butter, dribbled across the oysters, and bake at 400 for 15 minutes.

CHAPTER 5

. . . IS ANOTHER'S MEAT

For the quick gourmet chef, meat is sometimes a problem —so many of the most delicious dishes seem to require hours of simmering time.

When minutes matter, it often seems that meat is limited to lamb chops and steak, and as anyone knows who has tried it, it is possible to become jaded with filet mignon six nights in a row!

While steak is the greatest quick-cooking meat, there are others, and a real gourmet enjoys all of them. But first comes the steak, and a perfectly cooked steak depends upon three things: thickness of meat, true heat of the broiler, and your personal taste.

Real gourmets eat their steaks rare to blood-rare; well-done beef is only for pot roasts.

Many supposedly-tender cuts such as sirloin and porter-house can be made foolproof by an unseasoned meat tenderizer—to be sprinkled on and rubbed in about half an hour before cooking. This will not be necessary if you are lucky enough to have a butcher who hangs his own meat; very few do—and when they do, you pay accordingly.

Nothing is more critical than steak cookery because split seconds matter. A general rule for a 1-inch steak is: a 500 broiler, meat placed one inch below flame, broil 5 minutes on one side; turn over and broil 3 minutes on the other side. Remove steak *immediately;* a steak is one dish that cannot be "kept hot," for every extra minute of heat will destroy the perfect degree of done-ness for your taste.

Personal experimentation will be necessary for steaks, how-ever: perhaps yours is a gas-fired broiler and the thermostat may be slightly off; or your personal taste may be for more red than pink (or vice versa). Armed with a kitchen timer, you must define the exact number of minutes for the exact thickness of steak to produce the result *you* like best.

53

FILET MIGNON, TOURNEDOS and CHATEAUBRIAND

These are all prime beef tenderloin, differing only in size and presentation. Beef tenderloin *needs* nothing but a session beneath a broiler flame—but responds to many sauces and marinades.

Filet Mignon is a *slice* of tenderloin, and absolutely its own excuse for its price. It should be cut ¾ to an inch thick, weigh about half a pound per serving, and it should not be trimmed of whatever fat it possesses. A filet mignon is always broiled.

Tournedos are created by trimming and shaping the entire beef tenderloin into a long roll, wrapped in bacon strips or thin slabs of beef suet, securely tied in place. The Tournedos are then sliced evenly to your order in thicknesses of one or two inches. Customarily they are sauteed in butter or olive oil, and served with fancy sauces and garnishes.

Chateaubriand is a thick hunk of beef tenderloin in one piece, weighing one or two pounds. It is grilled or sauteed before slicing into serving portions. Expensive to buy in a restaurant, it's none too cheap to prepare at home—because the risk of failure is high. A true Chateaubriand must be well-browned but not charred on the outside; pinkish-red and warmed through, yet not raw at the center . . . and this ain't easy!

FILET MIGNON

A slice of beef tenderloin may be anointed with prepared mustard (Bahamian or Dijon); chutney juice; coarse-ground pepper; painted delicately with Kitchen Bouquet mixed in water. . . .

It can be anointed before cooking and basted as it is turned over during broiling, with a melted butter sauce containing: garlic; herbs (parsley, tarragon, chives, chervil); spices (nutmeg, cinnamon, ginger—but *never* cloves); grated lemon and orange peel . . .

It can be broiled *au naturel* and served with table sauces

from Bearnaise to Diable, Robert, Madeira or plain horse-radish. . . .

Aside from disastrous over-cooking, there is not really any-thing that can ruin a filet mignon—except a coating of mashed bananas and ground peanuts. . . .

For the simplest possible FILET MIGNON CHEZ VOUS: broil your filet to taste; place on the serving plates and smear with a generous tablespoon of butter per each. Douse with a tablespoon of Worcestershire Sauce. As this melts and runs together about the hot steak, it will blend with meat juices and no other table sauce will be needed.

TOURNEDOS BEARNAISE

Beef tenderloin on toast, with a traditional sauce.

Cook 4 tournedos in butter, place on small slices of but-tered toast (crusts removed), add 2 or 3 tablespoons of Bear-naise sauce on top of each tournedo—and serve extra Bear-naise sauce in a warmed sauce boat.

TOURNEDOS ROSSINI

Beef tenderloin on toast spread with pate de foie gras, topped by pan gravy.

4 tournedos cooked in butter to your taste	4 mushroom caps
	1 sliced truffle
4 slices of pate de foie gras (neatly cut from a chilled tin)	½ cup bouillon
	1 T meat glaze
	1 T sherry
2 T Madeira wine	Watercress garnish

Cook the tournedos in butter to your own taste, and re-move to a warmed platter. Saute mushroom caps gently for 5 minutes (in butter) while the tournedos are cooking, and prepare 4 slices buttered toast (crusts removed).

To the meat pan, add 4 neat slices of pate de foie gras and 1 minced truffle, and heat very gently in the meat drip-pings. Place the foie gras on the toast, top with the tournedos and a bit of minced truffle. Keep warm.

Deglaze the pan by adding the bouillon mixed with meat glaze and sherry, and the Madeira, and scraping down all the good brown bits of meat from the sides of the pan. Blend it all as smoothly as possible, pour over the tournedos, garnish with bunches of watercress.

CHATEAUBRIAND PARISIENNE

Beef tenderloin sauteed in onion-wine sauce, served with fancy vegetables.

1¾ pound beef tenderloin, in one piece, trimmed of fat and skin

½ pound butter

8 mushrooms, separated (caps left whole; stems sliced)

1 cup dry white wine

2 T minced fresh parsley

1 tsp tarragon

½ crumbled bay leaf

1 pinch of thyme

juice of half a lemon

1 tsp salt

½ tsp pepper

1 package frozen artichoke hearts

1 large tin small boiled potatoes

Melt 2 T butter in a frying pan over high flame; when golden brown, sear the steak quickly on both sides. Reduce heat and cook 10-12 minutes on each side over the low flame. Remove to a heated serving dish.

Meanwhile, cook and drain artichokes. In a separate frying pan, melt 2 T butter, add artichokes and mushroom caps, and saute very gently for 10 minutes.

Simultaneously, drain the tin of potatoes and place in a shallow baking dish with 2 T melted butter. Shake until thoroughly coated. Sprinkle with parsley and dust with paprika. Place in a 450 oven for about 10 minutes, or until lightly browned. . . . These are Potatoes Noisette. Shake the pan occasionally in the oven, to turn the potatoes over so they will brown evenly.

Sauce:

When the Chateaubriand is cooked to your taste, discard most of the pan fat, retaining only about a tablespoon. Add

½ tsp tarragon and stir with a wooden spoon. Add wine, thyme, bay leaf, and sliced mushroom stems, and cook until the sauce reduces to about half its volume, stirring constantly. Add 2 T butter cut in small pieces, and shake the pan back and forth until it melts. Finish with the juice of half a lemon, parsley and the remaining tarragon.

To Serve:

Place the Chateaubriand in the center of the serving platter, surround with artichokes and potato balls, and distribute mushroom caps on top. Pour some of the sauce over the meat, serve the rest in a separate sauce boat, and slice the meat in ¾-inch sections at table.

BEARNAISE SAUCE

The great traditional French steak sauce. . . .
While this is available in jars at gourmet food shops, it is not too difficult to make at home.

1 cup white wine	½ tsp chervil
1 T tarragon vinegar	2 crushed peppercorns
1 T minced shallots (or scallions)	3 egg yolks
	½ pound melted butter

Combine the wine, vinegar, shallots, chervil and peppercorns and cook briskly over a hot flame, until the liquid boils down to ⅔ its original volume. Cool slightly, add egg yolks and melted butter very gradually and alternately—stirring constantly and vigorously.

The sauce should end with the consistency of heavy cream —and because egg yolks differ in size, you may not need all the melted butter . . . add it sparingly after you've incorporated the eggs, and do not try to make the sauce absorb any more butter than it needs for a smooth texture. Blend thoroughly over a very low heat, strain through a fine sieve and decorate with a dash of paprika and a teaspoon of finely minced fresh parsley.

VEAL PARMIGIANA

Thin-sliced veal, topped with a tomato-cheese sauce.

This recipe will take every second of your 30-minute allotment, but it *can* be done—just . . .

4 veal cutlets—pounded thin by the butcher (you will need 2 pounds of meat by weight)

2 eggs, beaten with salt and pepper to taste

¾ cup bread crumbs

4 T grated Parmesan cheese

1 cup tomato sauce

thin slices of Mozzarella cheese

3 T olive oil

Dip the pounded veal cutlet pieces in beaten egg, then in crumbs and Parmesan cheese, and saute in hot olive oil until golden brown (about 10 minutes). Meanwhile heat the oven to 375.

Transfer the browned cutlets to a shallow baking pan, pour the tomato sauce over them, top with Mozzarella cheese slices and a sprinkling of grated Parmesan.

Bake for about 15 minutes, until the cheese melts and browns.

CHINESE PEPPER STEAK

A quick-cookery Oriental version of round steak, very simple to prepare at the last moment.

1¼ pound of round steak, in one piece

2 T olive oil

2 T minced onion

1 clove minced garlic

2 *large* sliced green peppers

½ cup sliced celery

1 tsp soy sauce

3 tsp cornstarch mixed in 2 T water

1 cup consomme

Slice the round steak in thin diagonal slivers—as though cutting a London Broil. Sear in hot olive oil. Add onion, garlic, seeded sliced peppers and celery, plus ½ cup of consomme.

Cover the pan, reduce heat and cook 5 minutes.

Add cornstarch and water mixture, stirring vigorously—

and more consomme if needed to make a smooth sauce. Add the soy sauce, and simmer 5 minutes more.

Serve at once with boiled rice.

BOEUF STROGANOFF

This is the great traditional Russian method of preparing beef tenderloin—simple to make, but too rich for a hot night!

1½ pounds beef tenderloin, cut in thin strips	2 cups beef bouillon
1 T flour	3 T sour cream
2 T butter, plus 3 T	2 T tomato paste
	1 large grated onion

Make the sauce first: blend 2 T butter with flour until smooth, place over low heat, and *very* gradually add the bouillon—stirring constantly as the mixture thickens and removing any flour lumps. Bring to a boil and cook 2 minutes, add sour cream and tomato paste alternately, stirring constantly. Place over a very low heat and simmer; do not allow it to boil.

In a frying pan, brown the pieces of beef in butter and onion, for about 5 minutes; combine contents of meat pan with the sauce, and simmer the whole dish very very gently for 15 or 20 minutes. Serve with plenty of fluffy rice.

STEAK POIVRADE (Peppered Steak)

Entirely distinct from Chinese Pepper Steak, this is a traditional French preparation of steak with ground pepper.

2 pounds beef steak: porterhouse, sirloin, tenderloin or what you will	2 T olive oil
2 T *coarse-ground* pepper	½ tsp cornstarch dissolved in 1 T water
4 T butter	2 T cognac
	¼ cup bouillon

Sprinkle one tablespoon of pepper on each side of the steak, pressing it firmly into the meat.

Heat butter and oil in a very heavy frying pan until hot

but not brown; quickly sear the steak on both sides—to press the pepper grains into the flesh. Cook 3-5 minutes per side (or until done to your taste). Salt the steak lightly, and remove to a heated serving platter.

Mix cornstarch with water smoothly, and add to steak pan. Pour in the cognac and stir thoroughly, scraping down every bit of meat glaze from the sides and bottom of the pan. Add bouillon, cook very gently for 5 minutes, stirring occasionally, and pour over steak.

For quick cookery, beef is the best bet—lamb can only be prepared as lamb chops (and anyone knows how to cook *them*). Pork, whether chops or fillet, demands thorough slow cooking and although there are many good pork recipes that require no more than a few minutes to *prepare*, any of them will take an hour to cook.

Next to beef, then, we have veal—and various "meat extras" such as kidneys and sweetbreads.

LAMB KIDNEYS SAUTEED

The simplest kidneys in wine, to be served with fluffy rice.

12 lamb kidneys, split by the butcher	6 shallots, minced
	1 clove of garlic, pressed
4 T butter	2 T minced parsley
12 mushrooms, thinly sliced	½ cup white wine

Place kidneys in a bowl of cold water for 5-8 minutes; drain, strip off any remaining white membrane, and cut the kidneys in pieces.

Melt 3 T butter in a frying pan, saute kidneys for 5 minutes. Add mushrooms and shallots, garlic and parsley. Toss and turn the kidneys in the vegetable mixture, and as liquid boils, add wine together with a pinch of salt and pepper and remaining butter.

Cover and cook over a very moderate heat for 15 minutes.

ROGNONS DE VEAU (Veal Kidneys)

Delicately flavored, veal kidneys baked with a butter-wine sauce . . . to be served with fluffy rice.

4 veal kidneys, cut in half
¼ pound melted butter
2 T minced fresh parsley
½ tsp nutmeg
½ tsp cinnamon

8 fresh mushrooms
¼ cup Calvados (apple brandy) or plain Armagnac

Heat the oven to 400.

Soak kidneys in cold water, while you melt butter, add parsley, nutmeg, cinnamon, mushroom caps, and sliced mushroom stems. Simmer for 5 minutes. Set aside the mushroom caps.

Drain the kidneys, removing any bits of white membrane overlooked by the butcher, and spread them in a buttered shallow baking pan.

Top with half of the butter sauce and bake for 10 minutes.

Turn over the kidneys, top with the reserved mushroom caps, add remaining sauce, mixed with the Calvados or brandy, and continue to bake for 10 minutes.

WIENER SCHNITZEL

A traditional Austrian veal dish, of thin veal cutlets in a breaded sauce.

2 pounds veal cutlet, cut in serving pieces and pounded thin
2 eggs, beaten
½ cup flour, seasoned with 1 tsp salt, ½ tsp pepper

¾ cup fine bread crumbs
½ pound butter
4 T minced parsley
3 T lemon juice

Dip veal pieces into the flour mixture—then into the beaten egg—and then in bread crumbs. Be sure each piece is well-coated with crumbs. Saute in melted butter for about 15 minutes or until tender, turning very tenderly so that the crumb-coating will not break away from the meat.

Remove the veal to warmed plates, add lemon juice and parsley, blend well, and pour over the veal before serving.

Wiener Schnitzel a la Holstein is exactly the same—but is embellished with a fried egg atop each cutlet.

OISEAUX SANS TÊTES (Veal Birds)

Rolled veal slices, stuffed with ham and bread, cooked in a simple broth.

8 pieces of veal, flattened as for scallopini	1 raw scraped carrot
	¼ cup bread crumbs
4 slices thin cold boiled ham	3 T minced parsley
½ cup butter	1 stalk minced celery
2 chopped large onions, 1 large sliced onion	½ tsp poultry seasoning
	1 cup consomme

Melt ¼ cup of butter, add chopped onions, celery and parsley, and saute until soft but not browned. Add crumbs and poultry seasoning, mix well. If the stuffing seems too dry, add a few tablespoons of heavy cream or a dash of dry white wine.

Spread each veal slice with half a slice of the ham, top with stuffing. Roll up and tie firmly with string, tucking in the ends as neatly as a Macy package-wrapper.

Melt remaining butter in a pressure cooker, add sliced onion and carrot; brown veal birds on all sides. Add consomme and cook for 15 minutes at 10 pounds pressure.

SWEETBREADS (Riz de Veau)

The thymus gland of the calf is a great delicacy in France. It must always be precooked as follows (so that any sweetbread recipe inevitably must be 2-Step Cookery):

Blanch sweetbreads by covering with cold water, adding 2 T white vinegar and bring to a boil. Reduce heat sharply and simmer for 20 minutes. Then drain, and plunge the sweetbreads into *icy-cold water* (sacrifice a tray of ice cubes, if you must, to pack about the sweetbreads). Let stand until cool enough to handle; trim away any tubes or membranes, slice sweetbreads in half—or in thick slices—depending on the recipe ahead. Wrap carefully and store overnight (but no longer) in the refrigerator.

Frozen sweetbreads exist in the West; in the East, where French gastronomy is more general, sweetbreads are only to be had from first-class meat markets at a shocking price—but worth it, of course, if you favor *la haute cuisine*. Every little French restaurant serves:

RIZ DE VEAU VIRGINIE

Sweetbreads atop ham, atop toast, and covered with a rich cream sauce.

2 pairs of sweetbreads, cooked, separated and split in half

4 ham slices

8 mushroom caps

2 cups rich cream sauce (made from condensed chicken soup thinned with ¾ cup heavy cream)

2 T minced fresh parsley

2 T minced green pepper

2 minced shallots or scallions, sauteed in 1 T butter

4 slices hot buttered toast cut in strips

Heat the oven to 450.

Saute pepper, shallots and mushrooms in butter gently until soft (about 5 minutes). Do not brown.

Combine 1½ tins cream of chicken condensed soup with ¾ cup of heavy cream in a double boiler top. Add sauteed vegetables and simmer sauce gently, adding a little milk if needed to thin sauce. Prepare the buttered toast strips; place them in a buttered shallow baking dish. Top with a neat slice of ham, and place half a sweetbread on the ham. For ease in serving, make four distinct portions—or prepare in individual ramekins.

Pour sauce over the ham-sweetbread mixture, sprinkle with parsley, and bake for 10 minutes or until lightly browned.

Because of their delicate flavor, wine can overpower sweetbreads, and no more than a tablespoon or two should ever be used in the sauce. The simplest preparation for sweet-breads (after blanching) is

RIZ DE VEAU CHEZ VOUS

2 pairs of blanched sweet-breads, cut in half
¼ pound melted butter
1 T white wine

1 T minced fresh parsley
¼ cup slivered or coarsely chopped Macadamia nuts or almonds

Place sweetbreads in a shallow greased baking dish, combine melted butter, wine and parsley, pour over sweetbreads, and bake 5 minutes in a 375 oven. Carefully turn over the sweetbreads, baste with the sauce, sprinkle with nuts, and bake another 5 to 10 minutes, or until nuts are lightly browned.

HAM

Ham is a very *positive* meat.

A slice of ham can be baked in practically anything, and the thinner the slice (though not less than ¾ inch), the quicker the cooking.

Ham goes with *strong* spices, such as cloves, allspice and nutmeg. It responds happily to a tin of any kind of fruit juice from papaya, to guava, to peach nectar; it also enjoys a milk bath, dusted with cloves . . . or it can be combined with a tin of almost any kind of fruit (including the juice).

Pineapple is traditional but uninteresting to a gourmet; try tinned figs, or apricots, or boysenberries, or grape juice . . . or anything at all *but* pineapple.

A slice of ham can be baked in beer or ale—or Coca Cola —but add ¼ cup of plain water to prevent any gummy residue that might toughen the ham slice.

Madeira wine and raisins go with baked ham, but otherwise a ham slice responds to few wine or butter basting sauces. You may use a split of champagne, if you like, but all the other wines and sauces are apt to be overpowered by the salt ham taste.

Nevertheless, ham is a universal favorite—and a fine standby for the quick gourmet chef. Remember only: keep it moist, make it sweet or very plain; *do not use* delicate or subtle flavors in sauces because the salt in the ham will kill the taste.

To serve four people, you will need a 2-lb slice of ham . . . plus whatever juices or spices you choose . . . and simply bake in a 400 oven for 30 minutes.

CHAPTER 6

CHICKEN

Chicken is a most rewarding dish, with which you can do practically anything, at any moment, in any way. William Randolph Hearst made it a rule that in every one of his numerous homes, there should ALWAYS be a cold roast chicken in the icebox. He might not visit that particular home for two years . . . but such was his power that 365 days of every year, a chicken was roasted tenderly and placed in readiness for his coming. . . .

Although the story goes that Mr. Hearst's servants grew very tired of eating up cold chickens, there is little doubt that under ordinary circumstances anyone would feel himself a millionaire if he could only open his refrigerator at any moment to discover within—a cold roast chicken!

Chicken, like shrimp, is good for any course but dessert. It can be absolutely plain-cooked (boiled, broiled, steamed, roasted) or it can be entirely a matter of its sauce . . . and almost nothing responds so amiably to the window-dressing of herbs, spices, wines, sweet and sour, minced vegetables and all the other gourmet tricks.

Chicken dishes, for this reason, often *seem* similar . . . because many of them start with disjointing and browning broiler sections. For instance:

CHICKEN NICOISE, NANTAISE, BENEDICTINE

In these great French dishes, all depends on the end-flavor you desire, for all are merely special sauces for sauteed chicken.

All chicken dishes will require every scrap of your quick-cookery time allowance—plus an **extra** 5 or 10 minutes sometimes, to create a really tender piece of chicken (depending on the bird).

In each dish, the first step is to brown chicken parts. If you start with the entire small chicken, set aside neck and back sections which merely take space in the pan and are not too rewarding on the plate. If possible, buy the chicken parts you personally prefer, whether breasts or thighs and legs.

To Start the Dish

Wipe chicken sections on paper toweling, melt ¼ cup butter in a large frying pan, and brown the chicken over medium-high heat. Reduce the flame, cover tightly and continue to cook chicken while making the sauces.

CHICKEN NICOISE

Baked chicken with olive-tomato sauce.

Nice is a southern French city; its cooking is closer to Italy than Paris. For this dish, brown chicken parts in a mixture of 2 T olive oil and 2 T butter. Remove to an ovenproof dish with ¼ cup of fat, and bake tender in a 375 oven for about 15 minutes, basting once or twice, using pan juices.

Meanwhile, prepare the sauce, as follows:

1 yellow onion, chopped	½ crumbled bay leaf
1 clove garlic, minced	1 pinch each: rosemary, summer savory, tarragon
24 pitted black olives	
8 small tomatoes, peeled and coarsely cut	2 T flour
	4 cooked artichoke hearts, coarsely cut
1 cup dry white wine	
4 T tomato sauce	

In a separate pan, heat 1 tablespoon of olive oil and brown onion and garlic; sprinkle with flour and cook gently until golden brown, adding a little more olive oil if needed. Add the wine, tomatoes, artichoke hearts and olives; season with herbs, and simmer over lowest possible heat for 20 minutes.

Pour the sauce over chicken and return to the oven for another 10 minutes before serving.

CHICKEN NANTAISE

Chicken in a creamy onion-mushroom sauce, with wine.

Sauce:

½ cup dry white wine
½ tsp vinegar
2 small peeled chopped tomatoes
2 small tins boiled onions, drained

½ pound mushrooms, coarsely cut
3 T heavy cream
1 T chopped fresh parsley
salt, pepper, paprika

For this dish, brown chicken parts in ¼ cup butter for 10 minutes. Add the drained tiny white onions and mushrooms and simmer in a covered pan, for 15 minutes.

Drain off most of the pan fat (leave about a tablespoon), stir in wine and vinegar, add chopped tomatoes and cook for 5 minutes.

Remove chicken and vegetables to a heated serving plate; add cream to the pan sauce, blend thoroughly and cook for 3 minutes.

Strain the sauce over chicken, top with chopped parsley and a sprinkle of paprika.

CHICKEN BENEDICTINE SAUCE

A creamy liqueur-flavored sauce for the chicken. . . .

½ pound mushrooms quartered
¼ cup heavy sweet cream

salt, pepper
2 T Benedictine

Brown chicken parts with salt and pepper in melted butter; cover and simmer for 15 minutes. Add mushrooms and simmer 10 minutes.

Remove to a warmed serving plate.

Discard all but a tablespoon of the cooking fat, add ¼ cup heavy cream and Benedictine liqueur. Stir smooth over low heat for a few minutes, and pour over the chicken just before serving.

CHICKEN BRANDADO

A richly sauced, brandy-flamed chicken dish.

Chicken sections for 4 serving portions (breast meat, legs and thighs, or what you like)
¼ cup butter
2 cloves garlic, sliced

1 cup white wine
½ cup brandy
1 cup heavy cream
2 egg yolks
salt, pepper, and ¼ tsp nutmeg

Saute chicken pieces in butter and garlic slices for 15 minutes, turning to brown thoroughly. Remove garlic and discard.

Add wine and brandy, raise heat to warm alcohol and flame the liquor, shaking pan vigorously until brandy stops burning.

Reduce heat to medium, cover pan and simmer for 15 minutes until chicken is tender, stirring occasionally.

Remove chicken to heated platter. Add cream, salt, pepper, nutmeg, and egg yolks (slightly beaten) to pan juices, stir constantly and bring to a boil. Pour over chicken before serving.

ARROZ CON POLLO and CHICKEN CACCIATORE

These are Spanish and Italian versions of chicken. Both recipes include tomatoes, but the Spanish version adds rice and colors it bright yellow with a touch of saffron.

Arroz con Pollo (pronounced arROTH conPOYo)

2 thin sliced yellow onions
4 T olive oil
6 shallots or scallions, minced
Chicken parts suitable for 4 (breasts, thighs and legs —or chicken wings, if you're in a mood to save money)
½ cup seasoned flour (1 tsp salt, ½ tsp pepper, ¼ tsp chervil, ⅛ tsp each of cumin powder and garlic powder)
1 bay leaf
2 T minced parsley
½ tsp saffron, steeped in a tablespoon hot water
2 cups consomme
1 large tin of drained tomatoes
2 cups quick-cooking rice
2 sweet green peppers
½ cup sherry

Saute onions and shallots in olive oil. Dredge chicken in seasoned flour and brown completely in pan with onions. Reduce heat slightly, add tomatoes, bay leaf, parsley and consomme plus saffron. Cover tightly and simmer 15 minutes. Add sliced seeded green sweet pepper and rice, and simmer 10 minutes, or until chicken is tender.

Finish the dish by stirring in the sherry and blending with the sauce.

Chicken Cacciatore (pronounced catchyaTAURray)

Italian chicken stew.

1 large sliced onion
4 T olive oil
suitable chicken parts for 4 (breasts, thighs, and legs)
½ cup seasoned flour (1 tsp salt, ½ tsp pepper, ½ tsp Marjoram, ⅛ tsp garlic powder)
2 cups canned tomatoes
1 cup coarsely chopped sweet green peppers (seeded)
½ cup white wine

Saute onion in 2 tablespoons of olive oil, while you toss chicken parts in a brown-paper bag with seasoned flour. Add chicken (floured) and remaining oil and brown. Add tomatoes and peppers, cover and saute 20 minutes over medium heat, stirring occasionally. Add wine, salt and pepper to taste, and cook again gently for 10 minutes or until tender.

ROAST CHICKEN STUFFINGS

Roast chicken is always roast chicken, unless you spend your ingenuity on a basting sauce—but the plainest little pullet can rise to great heights by its stuffing.

A roast chicken, however small, will still take most of an hour, and there is nothing to do about this—aside from offering guests an extra drink and special canapes.

To cut cooking time slightly, however, you should choose two very small chickens rather than the elegant capon; make the stuffing beforehand and leave the birds ready to GO. If time will really be at a premium, you may dare to precook your birds for 10 or 15 minutes—in which case, wrap them in aluminum foil to prevent over-browning of the skin before final cooking.

Stuffing #1 (a sweet-flavored Greek-Albanian stuffing)

1½ cups prepared package stuffing (or cubed stale bread)
½ cup butter
¼ cup each: seedless raisins and currants

2 T each: chopped black walnuts, chopped almonds, pignolias, hazelnuts (or plain walnuts and pecans)
¼ cup sugar
¼ cup consomme

Saute bread crumbs in melted butter for 5 minutes; add all other ingredients and mix thoroughly, adding more consomme if the stuffing seems too dry for your taste.

Stuffing #2 (Chestnut stuffing, traditional American style)

2 tins plain cooked chestnuts (take care! You do *not* wish the chestnuts intended for dessert sauces.)
3 shallots, chopped
2 T butter
½ lb sausage meat
1 tsp chives
¾ cup prepared bread crumb stuffing
2 T minced parsley
½ cup brandy
¼ tsp marjoram

Saute shallots in butter, add sausage meat, parsley and chives.

Cook 5 minutes gently, stirring with a fork to keep sausage crumbs separate.

Coarsely chop half the chestnuts; grind the other half.

Combine all ingredients and mix well, adding the brandy last to moisten the stuffing.

Stuffing #3 (for squabs)

2 small tins wild rice—*thoroughly* drained
1 tablespoon chopped fresh parsley
2 finely sliced onions
1 teaspoon sage
½ cup butter
¼ cup minced celery
½ cup consomme, 1 teaspoon salt, ¼ tsp pepper

Saute onions in melted butter until golden; add all other ingredients, and toss about rapidly over medium heat until well blended.

CHICKEN CUTLETS KIEV

Rich and Russian (White Russian, obviously!), these are deep-fried buttery chicken breasts.

2 whole chicken breasts, split in half
4 T *very* cold sweet butter
2 beaten eggs
bread crumbs
hot frying fat
4 wooden skewers (resembling drumsticks)

72

Remove skin from chicken and take the meat from the bone. Flatten severely with the flat side of a meat cleaver.

Place a tablespoon of very cold butter at one end of the chicken fillet and roll slightly; insert a skewer and continue rolling to the end of the slice, securing firmly with thread.

Heat the frying fat to 370.

Slightly beat eggs, and dilute with 1 scant T water; dip the rolled cutlet in egg and in bread crumbs. Fry in the hot fat.

Unless the chicken cutlet is very thick, 5 minutes should be sufficient cooking time.

MOO GOO GAI PAN (Chinese Chicken Almond)

2 whole raw chicken breasts, removed from the bone and cut in fine strips

4 T olive oil

2 cups bamboo shoots

2 cups diced celery

1 cup shredded Chinese cabbage

1 cup water chestnuts, sliced

½ cup blanched, halved almonds

2 T soy sauce

2 tsp Monosodium Glutamate (Accent powder)

3 cups chicken consomme

4 T cornstarch, mixed smooth in 3 T cold water

Fry chicken strips in olive oil over high heat, stirring constantly for 5 minutes.

Add everything else but cornstarch mixture, cover the pan and steam over medium heat for 5 minutes.

Stir in the cornstarch-water paste, using high heat and stirring vigorously and constantly to thicken the dish. Cook for 5 minutes. Serve at once with plenty of boiled rice.

CHICKEN TETRAZZINI

A delicious leftover chicken preparation, with the rich sauce beloved of the great Italian diva, Luisa Tetrazzini.

2 cups cooked chicken meat, cut in pieces
1 can condensed cream of chicken soup
½ cup thin cream
½ pound mushrooms
6 T butter
3 T sherry
salt, pepper, ¼ tsp nutmeg
½ cup grated Parmesan cheese
½ cup sliced truffles
2 cups cooked spaghetti

Saute coarse-cut mushrooms in butter over a low flame until soft and slightly browned (8 minutes). Meanwhile, cook ½ pound spaghetti in rapidly boiling salted water until tender. Drain and keep warm.

Combine soup, cream, sherry, salt, pepper, and nutmeg in a double boiler and heat gently, for 8 minutes.

Add half the sauce to mushrooms and drained spaghetti; mix the other half with chicken and truffles.

Place the spaghetti in a buttered shallow baking dish (or distribute among four individual ramekins); make a well in the center of the spaghetti and pour chicken mixture into it.

Top with grated cheese, and brown lightly for 10 minutes in a moderate 375 oven.

CHICKEN DIVAN

Leftover chicken slices, on a bed of broccoli, topped by a rich cream sauce.

1 box frozen broccoli
1 tsp Worcestershire Sauce
3 T sherry
½ cup heavy whipped cream
½ cup Hollandaise sauce
1 cup grated Parmesan cheese
¼ tsp nutmeg
1 tin condensed cream of chicken soup
½ cup milk
4 large slices of cooked chicken

Heat the oven to 500.

Place broccoli in boiling water and slightly undercook (10 minutes).

Sauce: heat condensed chicken soup and milk, plus nutmeg, sherry and Worcestershire Sauce in a double boiler, stirring smooth. Simmer for 10 minutes, remove from fire and stir in ½ cup prepared Hollandaise sauce.

Drain broccoli, arrange on a shallow baking dish, sprinkle with ½ cup of grated cheese and top with chicken slices. (Arrange for easy serving in 4 portions.)

Fold whipped cream into the warm sauce, pour over the chicken, top with remaining cheese and broil until the top is lightly browned, keeping the dish about 5 inches below broiler flame, for 10-15 minutes.

CHAPTER 7

SPECIALITÉS DE LA MAISON

A *specialité de la maison* is simply the main dish *you* prepare best.

It may be tripe or Chateaubriand; a special sauce for codfish cakes or Lobster Thermidor; it can be your own trick of preparing hash, stew, or a slumgullion of tasty leftovers—or it may be a recipe used only for champagne occasions.

No matter what its ingredients, a *Specialité* is simply the recipe you have made your very own, either by embroidering on a basic dish, or by learning to create a traditional recipe with the definitive touch.

But it is always the dish you have made so many times that you scarcely need to glance at the cookbook—and the mere suggestion that this might be scheduled for tonight's menu will brighten all eyes (and increase the saliva).

For instance—spaghetti. Despite the calories, everyone enjoys it, if the sauce is special . . . and nothing is simpler than to create your own variation of . . .

BASIC SPAGHETTI SAUCE

2 T olive oil
1 clove garlic
2 large yellow onions, thin-sliced
½ green pepper, seeded and thin-sliced
2 or 3 stalks of celery, coarsely cut
1 tsp oregano

½ pound ground beef
2 tins condensed tomato soup
1 small tin tomato paste
2 small tins of mushroom "bits and pieces" (or ¼ pound fresh mushroom stems, thin sliced)
1 C water

Saute onion, celery and green pepper in olive oil for 3 minutes; add ground meat (the cheapest grade is advisable here—because its fat content adds to the cooking liquid). Brown and pull apart meat into crumbs with a fork.

Add soup, oregano, mushrooms and tomato paste—plus a little water if needed to keep the sauce from being too thick.

Cover and simmer over the lowest possible heat for 25 minutes, checking occasionally to be sure it does not stick to the pan.

Serve on thin spaghetti—which cooks while the sauce is maturing. Place plenty of grated Parmesan cheese on the table, to sprinkle on top.

This is the basis for your own invention. You may add a cup of mixed leftover cooked vegetables; this not only extends the sauce for unexpected guests but also cleans out the refrigerator painlessly. . . . Beans of all sorts, peas, carrots, Brussels sprouts, cauliflower . . . anything and everything is permissible in a good spaghetti sauce.

SPAGHETTI CARUSO substitutes ½ a pound of fresh chicken livers for the ground beef . . . and CLAM SAUCE is rapidly made by using a tin of minced clams (with their juice) instead of meat.

Cooked lobster meat, crabmeat, cleaned shrimps, or diced chicken can also be substituted for the raw ground beef— or you may use 2 dozen well scrubbed Cherrystone clams or fresh mussels, distributed atop the sauce for the final ten minutes of cooking.

Traditional seasoning is oregano, but marjoram, basil, rosemary or summer savory will do equally well. A teaspoon of celery seeds can replace celery stalks, and ¼ tsp garlic powder can replace the minced garlic clove.

For the palate geared to hot seasonings, add a tablespoon of Worcestershire Sauce, or a tablespoon of "hot" catsup.

OLLA PODRIDA—*the Spanish equivalent of a New England boiled dinner, although fancier. This requires two steps in cooking*

½ pound each: veal cutlet, round steak, lamb chops (boned), cooked ham
1 chicken breast
2 smoked sausages (Spanish *chorizos*, if possible—or sweet Italian sausage)
3 T olive oil
1 tin of cooked chick peas (Garbanzos beans)
2 chopped onions
2 minced cloves of garlic
1 tsp salt
½ tsp pepper
2 quarts water
1 cup shredded white cabbage
½ package frozen peas
½ package frozen string beans
1 large cucumber, peeled and sliced
1 head of lettuce, coarsely shredded

Step #1:

Brown the beef, veal, lamb and chicken in hot olive oil. Combine browned meats in a pressure cooker, with ham, sliced sausages, onions, garlic, salt and pepper, cover with water and cook for 30 minutes at 10 pounds pressure. Allow pressure to decrease normally, and store in refrigerator overnight.

Step #2:

Cook cabbage, peas and beans for 10 minutes in 2 cups of stock, while reheating stew separately.

Add drained chick peas to the stew.

Add lettuce and cucumber to cabbage mixture and cook another 10 minutes.

To serve:

Place meats and chick peas on a platter; vegetables in another platter; combine all cooking juices in a soup tureen.

Provide each guest with an old-fashioned flat-lipped soup plate and a salad-sized plate, and allow him either to combine everything in the soup dish or eat broth separately from meat and vegetables.

A good green salad and plenty of crusty French bread completes the meal.

MUSHROOMS FARCIS *Anything "farcis" means "stuffed"*

12 *immense* mushrooms—separate the caps, and chop the stems finely

¼ cup finely minced leftover chicken

1 clove pressed garlic (or a dash of garlic powder)

2 tablespoons chopped fresh parsley

2 eggs

¼ cup butter

salt and pepper

Saute chopped mushroom stems in the butter for 10 minutes, add garlic, parsley and seasonings. Mix with minced chicken, and lightly beaten eggs. Pile into mushroom caps. Dust the tops with a few bread crumbs, a teaspoon of grated Parmesan cheese, and a dash of paprika. Place caps in a buttered baking pan, and cook 15 minutes in a moderate oven.

FROGS' LEGS

The small Eastern variety of frogs' legs are *always* preferable in delicacy of taste to the big western and mid-Western frog saddles, and for quick-cookery, only the small frogs' legs can be prepared in a short time. The large legs need to be soaked in milk or a wine marinade for several hours before cooking.

Frogs' legs are particularly a French specialty, and although they are classed with fish and seafood dishes, actually taste very much like chicken.

Best known preparation is probably

FROGS' LEGS PROVENCALE

The legs are sauteed until brown, and served with a foaming butter sauce, heavily seasoned with garlic.

2 pounds small frogs' legs	2 T minced fresh parsley
5 T butter	3 large cloves of garlic, finely
2 T lemon juce	minced

Wash the frogs' legs, wipe dry, and saute in 2 tablespoons of butter until they are a golden brown (about 10-15 minutes).

Remove to a heated serving dish, sprinkle with the lemon juice and parsley. Add remaining butter and garlic to the frying pan, stir over medium heat until the butter browns slightly and foams—pour the foaming butter-garlic sauce generously over the frogs' legs and serve at once.

A second well-known preparation for frogs' legs is

FROGS' LEGS POULETTE

Traditionally, this is a dish of the meat from cooked frogs' legs, in a rich cream sauce, served in patty shells or individual ramekins.

2 pounds of small frogs' legs	1 T minced fresh parsley
2 T butter	½ tsp salt
½ cup dry white wine	½ tsp sugar
1 small white onion, minced	¼ tsp pepper
1 small scraped carrot, minced	¼ tsp paprika
1 generous T flour	½ cup cream
1 T lemon juice	2 egg yolks

Wash and dry the frogs' legs, saute in butter with onion and carrot for 5 minutes, turning constantly. Sprinkle with the flour, add wine, lemon juice, salt, pepper and parsley. Bring to a boil, stirring constantly to prevent flour lumps; reduce the heat and simmer very gently for 15 minutes.

Remove frogs' legs from pan and keep warm.

At this point, traditionally, the meat is removed from the

bones and reheated in the sauce, to be served in individual portions—but for quick gourmet cookery, you may save time by serving the whole cooked legs in the sauce.

In either case, add cream, paprika and sugar to the pan sauce and blend well. Thicken with lightly beaten egg yolks, and pour over the frogs' legs on their serving dishes. Garnish with a sprinkle of minced fresh parsley and a dash of paprika.

ESCARGOTS (Snails)

Snails are another typically French gourmet dish, but one that depends *entirely* upon the sauce, as snail meat itself is both leathery in texture and uninterestingly tasteless.

Snails are generally served in their shells, in special small pans; they should be served hot-hot-hot, and for ease in handling, it's worth while to buy the real snail tongs.

Any gourmet food store, as well as most supermarkets today, sells packaged snails—with or without shells. For an appetizer, 4 or 6 snails is the usual portion; as a main dish, serve a full dozen. Shells are easily soaked clean, to be retained from one meal to the next, and once you have sufficient small snail shells on hand, you can buy the canned cooked snails alone.

Escargots Bourguignonne is the most familiar recipe, and once you have mastered the method, you can invent your own personal sauce.

4 dozen snails, and 4 dozen snail shells
¾ cup butter
2 finely minced shallots
1 large (or 2 small) garlic cloves, peeled and pressed
1 T minced fresh parsley

1 tsp chervil
1 T minced fresh chives (or 1 tsp dried chives)
½ tsp salt, ¼ tsp pepper, ¼ tsp paprika
1 T brandy, or Burgundy (optional)

Drain the can of snails.
Heat the oven to 450.
Cream together: butter, herbs, seasonings, add the brandy or wine last, if you use it. Blend smoothly.

Put a tiny bit of the butter mixture in each snail shell, insert a snail and close the opening evenly with more of the creamed butter.

Arrange the snails in their pans—or standing upright in individual serving dishes.

Bake 6 or 7 minutes, until the snails are heated through and the butter melts.

Snails absolutely require crusty French or Italian bread, and a real gourmet literally mops up his snail pan sauce with his fingers.

Snails can also be prepared in advance and held in the refrigerator overnight until they are put in the oven—and in this case, you may make the sauce even more quickly by melting the butter and blending in your choice of herbs and seasonings. Dribble a bit of the melted butter into each snail shell, insert the snail and pour more melted butter sauce to fill the chinks to the top. Allow a good 10 minutes for baking snails that have come from the refrigerator.

SNAILS IN CREAM *Rich, but good*

4 dozen canned snails, well-drained

1 tin condensed mushroom soup

1 cup cream

1 minced onion

Combine all ingredients in the top of a double-boiler, stir smoothly, and simmer until hot and well-blended. Serve in 4 patty shells.

CHICKENBURGERS

Walter Winchell's favorite dish—a soft hash made from raw ground chicken . . .

2 cups ground raw chicken (the meat from 4 chicken breasts put through your grinder)

1 cup cream

1½ tsp salt

¼ tsp nutmeg

½ cup of bread crumbs

1 T minced parsley

Combine all ingredients—the mixture should be rather soft. Shape into four portions and coat with more bread crumbs.

Place on a lightly greased broiling pan, dot with bits of butter, and broil 8 or 9 minutes on each side.

Serve with SAUCE SUPREME, which is basically the old familiar white sauce enriched with mushrooms, cream and egg yolks . . . but a satisfactory approximation is quickly made as follows:

1 can condensed mushroom soup	2 T dry sherry
	1 minced truffle
1 cup thin cream	2 tsp lemon juice
1 lightly beaten egg yolk	½ tsp paprika

Combine soup and cream in the top of a double boiler, blend smooth. Add sherry, minced truffle, lemon juice and paprika and blend again. Finally, thicken with the egg yolk and serve handsomely, dribbled about the base of each chickenburger and sprinkled with fresh parsley or a colorful dash of paprika.

SQUABS

Pigeon squab is infinitely superior to chicken squab, but unless you live in the country, you may have to settle for the chicken.

Rock Cornish Game Hens are delicious, but it is not possible to do them justice in less than a full hour. A half-Game Hen, stuffed with wild rice, is sometimes available in a frozen foods department of good supermarkets; if you can find this, it can be cooked (well-basted with a butter sauce) in an electric oven or broiler—in about 30 minutes.

Fresh squab, whether pigeon or chicken, can be cooked more quickly if they are split—and it's customary to split them from the back to the breastbone without entirely cutting them apart. They are then flattened out, and sauteed on both sides in plenty of butter.

83

PIGEONNEAUX SMITANE

Sauteed squabs in a sour cream sauce.

4 squabs, split from the back and flattened for quick cooking
½ cup butter (sweet butter is preferable) + 2 T
1 T cognac
2 minced shallots
1 T fresh minced chives
4 mushrooms, coarsely cut

2 ripe tomatoes, peeled and coarsely cut
1 crumbled bay leaf
1 pinch thyme
1 tsp paprika
1 tsp summer savory
2 T dry white wine
1 cup heavy sour cream

Saute the flattened squabs in melted butter for 10 minutes.

Sprinkle with a tablespoon of good brandy, and saute for another ten minutes, turning the squabs frequently so they will brown attractively.

In a separate pan, melt 2 T butter, and very gently saute the shallots, chives, mushrooms, tomatoes, bay leaf, thyme, summer savory and paprika for 10 minutes. In another pan, scald the sour cream.

Transfer the browned squabs, plus enough pan juice to protect them from burning, to a casserole and place in a 350 oven.

Combine remaining pan juice from the squabs with the sauteed vegetables, add wine and scalded sour cream. Simmer for 8 minutes, stirring smoothly.

Finally pour over the cooked squabs on serving dishes.

PARTRIDGE

2 partridge—cleaned and wiped with a cloth. Do not wash!
3 raw onions
6 strips of bacon
2 T parsley flakes
2 bay leaves
2 tsp juniper berries

¼ tsp thyme
1 tsp salt
½ tsp pepper
½ lb butter, melted
2 tsp garlic powder
½ cup sliced mushrooms
12 whole green olives
Brandy

Pre-heat oven to 400. Wipe the partridges with a clean cloth, inside and out. Sprinkle with salt, pepper and thyme; combine juniper berries, 2 strips bacon, bay leaves, parsley, 1 tsp garlic powder and 1 coarsely sliced onion, and distribute between the two partridge cavities. Tie 2 strips of bacon around each partridge breast.

Place the partridges on their sides in a baking dish, and pour melted butter over them. Add sliced mushrooms, 2 coarsely sliced onions, olives and remaining tsp of garlic powder.

Bake for 30 minutes at 400, turning and basting every 5 minutes.

Meanwhile make the sauce: 2 T butter, 2 T minced parsley, ¼ tsp thyme, 2 minced shallots, ½ cup dry sherry. Stir briskly, and when it boils, pour over the partridge on the serving plates.

Finally, pour a pony of brandy over each serving portion, light and flame, serve as soon as flames die.

CHAPTER 8

GOURMET ORIENTALE

Oriental dishes have become increasingly well-known to Occidental palates. While we had always understood that time had no meaning whatever in the Orient, oddly enough most Chinese and Japanese cookery requires only minutes to prepare.

Presentation of a dish is much more important in the Orient than in even the fanciest gourmet restaurant of the West. In authentic Japanese or Chinese cookery, for instance, there are special—and very time-consuming—ways to cut and slice vegetables: some are supposed to resemble flowers and others should look like tiny fishes, and it is all very beautiful but in the last analysis, they still *taste* like carrots and peas. . . .

Generally speaking, Oriental cuisine is "innumerable variations on a single theme"—and the theme is rice. The variations are chicken, pork, beef, eggs, lobster and shrimps. Lamb, veal and ham practically are unknown in the Orient . . . but the East has things unknown to us, such as Korean shrimps which are infinitely superior to the fanciest Gulf prawns we have ever known.

While Oriental recipes are generally more highly seasoned and spiced than our western cookery, they are not necessarily *hot* in the sense of, say Mexican cookery. Many Eastern spices and herbs are more tasty than tangy, and although they may require a little caution until your palate is used to them, they are also a fertile field for experimentation . . . for as you learn their distinctive flavors, you will dare to add a pinch of this or that to one of your prized Occidental recipes—to create a totally new and delicious effect.

CURRY IN A HURRY

One of the most gourmet of all dishes is the curry.

Almost *anything* can be curried.

A good curry sauce is the definitive answer to leftovers; it is far more impressive than even your finest *pasta* dish in those difficult moments when cocktail guests are having such a good time they refuse to go home—and in order to feed your famished family, you are forced to offer "potluck" for everyone.

While the authentic East Indian curry takes hours to prepare, a gourmet effect can be produced in minutes with today's ingredients.

If you are not familiar with curry, it's wise to experiment as regards the amount of seasoning you personally prefer. Gourmets of long standing, and people who have lived in the Orient, usually like *lots* of curry, but for your first attempts, make it mild. With time, its odd musty flavor will appeal more and more, and you will find yourself increasing the amount gradually until you, too, are unsatisfied unless it takes the roof off your mouth.

Curry was admittedly originated as a substitute for refrigeration in the hot countries of the Orient. Its heavy spice not only disguised the taste of meats and poultry gone a bit "high," but provided a bulwark within the tummy against possible ptomaine.

Curry is generally available in powdered form; it also exists in paste form. Its basic ingredients are cumin, coriander, cardamom, cloves, mace, ginger, black pepper, Cayenne, dill, fenugreek (which is a hard seed with a pleasant smell that is also used in chutneys), and turmeric—which creates the characteristic mustard-yellow color.

For the gourmet chef, curry presents a wonderful field for exploration and experimentation. You may add as much plain turmeric as curry powder, to give an extra deep-yellow Oriental color to the dish. A ¼ tsp lovage will further enhance the flavor. Fish, eggs, all kinds of meats, and a great many vegetables can be curried, either alone or in combinations according to your fancy . . . and fruit curries are equally delicious.

The real Far Eastern touch depends upon side dishes, known as "sambals." There are at least twenty traditional varieties . . . plus whatever your own ingenuity and palate may dictate.

All curries are served with rice, which is the staple food of the Orient, replacing our bread.

Depending upon the number of sambals you serve with your curry, it is correctly called "Eight-boy Curry," "Eleven-boy Curry," etc., etc. . . . and that is because, in the old days of the British Raj and the East Indian planters, each sambal was served by a separate turbaned houseboy, dressed in a starched white tunic with high tight collar; it was sometimes the whim of the host to turban each boy in a color to match or complement the particular sambal he offered to the guests!

The traditional service of curry and the Javanese Rijstaffel is always basically the same: first, a plate before each guest; second, the bowls of fluffy hot rice; third, the curry sauces and hot main dishes, and lastly, the "sambals." But while formerly the host provided a servitor for each side dish —and even today, a Batavian hotel serves its Rijstaffel with 20 native boys each bearing a sambal dish in either hand!— your guests will be equally happy with as many accompaniments as can be tastefully displayed upon a "Lazy Susan!"

First—

The Curry Sauce:

1 tin condensed cream soup . . . mushroom, celery, asparagus, cream of vegetable, cream of chicken . . . the choice will depend on what is to be curried	⅛ tsp garlic powder
	½ green pepper, seeded and thinly sliced
	1 or 2 stalks of celery, chopped
	Curry powder—1 or 2 tablespoons
1 large onion, very thinly sliced	Turmeric—an amount equal to the curry powder
1 cup milk	Lovage—¼ tsp

Combine soup and milk in the top of a double boiler, mix smooth. Add all other ingredients and whatever is to be curried (meat, fish, vegetables, etc.). Stir thoroughly, cover and hold over hot water, stirring occasionally, for 30 minutes.

SAMBALS (side dishes)

Traditional	*For quick service*
Fresh grated coconut	A can or package of commercial coconut
Sauteed onion rings	
Pepper rings: both fresh green and sweet red peppers	A tin, or frozen package, of French fried onions
	Tinned pimiento, cut in very fine strips

Crisp-fried bacon, cut very finely

Chopped peanuts, either plain or salted

Hardboiled eggs: shell, separate whites from yolks and sieve. Serve with a pile of yolk in the center, surrounded by minced egg whites

Freshly grated orange and lemon peels—served in small individual dishes.

Cucumbers: Do *not* peel; scrub thoroughly, slice very thinly and marinate in Vinaigrette dressing. Serve chilled.

A mixture of freshly chopped parsley and chives

Coarsely cut firm cherry tomatoes

Seedless raisins, Sultanas, and currants—soaked in sherry and drained

Grapefruit and/or orange sections, soaked in sherry

Toasted slivered almonds, or chopped cashews

Finely chopped hazelnuts (or pistachio nuts)

Chutney

Preserved ginger, cut fine

Fruit sherbet (to cool the palate if the curry is *hot*)

Bombay Ducks—which are not poultry but salty dried East Indian fish, to be crumbled over the curry

Sauteed bananas: sprinkle bananas with sugar, fresh lime juice, grated nutmeg, and saute in butter until light brown

Peeled, coarsely cut sections of fresh ripe mangoes

Finely chopped *green* tomatoes, marinated in French
    dressing
Chopped preserved kumquats
Green tomato conserve
Grated bitter chocolate (particularly for fruit curries)
Minced fresh mint
Grated carrot mixed with a little grated white onion
Minced celery
Chopped sauteed mushrooms

Oh, sambals are endless! Your particular choice will depend
upon what is already part of the curry itself; the side dishes
should be selected to point up the basic flavors.

RICE

Today's packaged and quick-cooking rice makes curry
service an easy matter. Our personal preference is Minute
Rice, which can be made first and set aside to keep warm
while you give your attention to the main dish.

If you fancy the authentic Oriental preparation of rice, it
is still quite easy to make.

East Indian Rice

1 cup white long-grain rice	1 tsp lemon juice or mild
1 tsp salt	white vinegar
2 T butter	2½ cups water

Start the water in a deep saucepan, add salt, lemon juice
and butter, and bring to a boil—while you wash the rice very
thoroughly, to remove *all* the starch. Add the rice slowly to
the boiling water, bring once more to the boil, cover and
reduce heat sharply until the rice just simmers over the lowest
heat. When the rice is tender (about 15-20 minutes) drain
in a colander, cover with a clean dishtowel, and steam the
rice over hot water for 5 or 10 minutes. Do *not* rinse the rice
before the final steaming period. Do *not* peek during the
cooking period. Keep the heat very low to prevent sticking,

and do not stir or you will end with broken bits instead of
fluffy separate grains.

To serve rice with an Oriental look, pile it loosely in a
deep custard cup and unmold on the plate in a neat mound.

STEAMED RICE VARIATIONS

For 2 cups of steamed rice, add any of the following:

Malay Versions

1. finely chopped nuts—pignolias, cashews, pistachios,
   almonds . . . ½ cup
2. minced parsley—2 tablespoons
3. ½ drained can of pineapple bits, sauteed in 1 tablespoon of butter
4. 1 teaspoon turmeric

Indian Versions

1. Saute a minced onion in 2 tablespoons butter, sprinkle with ¼ teaspoon ground allspice, ¼ teaspoon
   cinnamon, 1 pinch each of ground cloves and garlic
   powder. Cook about 4 minutes, until onion is soft,
   and mix with steamed rice
2. ¼ cup slivered toasted almonds and ¼ cup Sultana
   raisins
3. ½ teaspoon of curry powder to 2 cups steamed rice

Bali

Add a tablespoon of curry powder to 2 cups steamed rice

East Africa

¼ cup each of chopped peanuts and currants

RIJSTAFFEL

This is the traditional Javanese dinner, which was developed in the great plantation days of the last century, by the Dutch planters who had scant amusement aside from eating, poor things. A complete Rijstaffel consists of ten or a dozen main dishes, mostly curries, and as many sambal dishes as one can think of. It bears witness to the era when servants, particularly in the Orient, were practically a penny a dozen . . . because traditional preparation and service will require a full day plus six extra hands.

However, some of the Rijstaffel main dishes can easily be made in a short time—to be accompanied, as always with mounds of fluffy rice and a few of the simplest sambals.

Nasi Goreng

East Indian fish and meat dish, highly spiced.

1 cup cooked chicken meat, cut in strips	4 tablespoons peanut or salad oil (not olive oil)
1 cup cooked shrimp, coarsely chopped	2 chopped onions
1 can crabmeat (drained and fibers removed, coarsely cut)	1 clove garlic, pressed
	1 tsp ground coriander
	½ tsp ground cumin
½ cup cooked ham cubes	¼ tsp ground chili peppers
1½ cups cooked rice	¼ tsp mace
	2 T peanut butter

First prepare quick-cooking rice and set aside to mature until needed. Leftover rice is excellent; in Java, the rice for Nasi Goreng is usually cooked the previous day, so that it will be very dry.

Next start the oil, add minced onions and garlic, and cook over a *very* low flame to prevent burning. Stir occasionally.

Prepare shrimp—cleaned frozen shrimp need only about 10 minutes to cook in boiling water to cover, and are better than tinned shrimps because they are more firm in texture.

While shrimp are boiling, cut up the chicken and ham; clean a can of crab meat (*Geisha* brand or similar) and shred in fairly large pieces.

Add rice to onions, and stir frequently until it browns.

Drain shrimp and cut coarsely. Add all the meat and fish, plus spices and peanut butter, to the rice and mix well. Cook gently, stirring constantly, over low heat for 10 minutes. Serve with several sambals, such as chutney, chopped raisins, sliced fresh banana, or grapefruit sections.

HATI HATI

Chicken livers, highly seasoned.

1 lb chicken livers, coarsely chopped
1 cup coconut
1 cup milk
3 T butter
1 small chopped onion
1 clove garlic, pressed
¼ tsp dried ground chili pepper

¼ cup ground almonds
2 T grated lemon rind fresh (1 tablespoon of powdered lemon rind)
2 tablespoons orange juice
½ tsp salt
1 Tamarind—*or* a tablespoon each of fresh lemon juice and plum jam

Combine coconut and milk in a saucepan, bring to a boil, remove from heat and leave for 15 minutes. Then press all the milk from the coconut; discard the pulp.

Melt butter, add onion, garlic and chili powder, and saute 5 minutes, stirring frequently. Add livers and saute for 10 minutes, turning occasionally. Add remaining ingredients, including coconut milk, cook over low heat for 10 minutes, stirring occasionally. Serve with rice.

BAKED SPICY FISH

4 fish fillets (sole, mackerel, or boned shad)
½ cup melted butter
3 T lemon juice
¼ cup soy sauce

¼ tsp ground chili peppers
1 tsp salt
¼ tsp pepper
2 pressed cloves of garlic

93

Mix salt, pepper and garlic together thoroughly and rub on both sides of fish fillets. Place in a buttered baking dish and bake 10 minutes in moderate (375) oven. Combine remaining ingredients in a butter melter, blend well and keep warm. Use about a third of it to baste the fish after ten minutes; continue to bake for another 20 minutes, basting and turning the fillets several times. Distribute the remaining warm sauce over the cooked fillets when you transfer them to serving plates, and accompany with steamed rice.

FRUIT CURRY (2-Step Cookery)

½ cup fresh ripe mango, cut coarsely

2 ripe peaches, peeled and sliced

1 cup fresh melon balls (or a defrosted package)

1 sliced banana

1 small drained tin of pineapple chunks

1½ cups Sauterne (or enough to cover fruit mixture in a bowl)

1½ cups chicken consomme

¼ cup each: chopped pistachio nuts (or almonds); Sultana raisins

1 tsp cornstarch, mixed in 1 T water

2 T curry powder

Grated coconut and cooked steamed rice

1. Combine all the fruits in a bowl, cover with Sauterne, and let stand for at least 2 hours in the refrigerator. If you prepare the fruit on the previous evening, sprinkle banana and peaches with the juice of a lemon and place them at the bottom of the bowl where they will be well-covered by the wine—to prevent unsightly blackening of the fruit.

2. Drain the fruit juice and wine, and return fruit to the refrigerator.

Prepare 2 cups quick-cooking rice and set aside to keep warm.

Combine 1½ cups of the wine with 1½ cups chicken consomme in a deep saucepan, and simmer for 10 minutes. Add nuts and raisins, and thicken the sauce with cornstarch dissolved in a little warm water. Stir smooth, and add a bit of the mixture to the curry powder to dissolve it; return curry to the sauce, and cook smoothly for 5 minutes.

To serve: apportion the chilled fruit over hot rice on each plate, cover with some of the hot sauce (placing the rest in a sauce pitcher on the table), sprinkle with coconut.

SUKIYAKI

This is properly pronounced "Skee*yaki*" and is the national dish of Japan. It should be prepared at table in a chafing dish, and much depends upon the artistry with which you cut and slice the ingredients, as well as the quick cooking.

4 T salad oil (wesson, sesame, peanut—for once you do not need pure olive oil!)
2 bunches scallions
1 green pepper, seeded
3 yellow onions
3 stalks celery
½ pound mushrooms
1 cup bamboo shoots
¼ cup sugar
¾ cup soy sauce
1 cup strong bouillon
1 cup shredded spinach
2 pounds sirloin steak
½ pound vermicelli, boiled and drained (or 1 cake soybean curd)
Sake or Sherry

First, you must cut the meat and vegetables prettily: The steak should be cut in thin slices, about 2 inches square by ½ an inch thick. The celery stalks should be cut on the diagonal; the mushrooms should be sliced from one side of the cap to the other—in such a way that, through the stem area, there will be thin umbrella-shaped pieces. If you can obtain genuine soybean curd, it is traditionally sliced ¼ inch thick.

Cut the green seeded pepper in rings.

Wash and shred the spinach coarsely (cabbage, either Chinese or white, can be substituted here).

Clean the scallions and cut them in 3-inch lengths, tops and all.

Peel and thinly slice the yellow onions.

Slice the bamboo shoots (drain them from a can).

Prepare a cup of strong bouillon (use 2 bouillon cubes).

All the above operations should be done in the kitchen.

The various ingredients are then distributed artistically in small groups on a large platter. For your first attempt, perhaps you will be wise to place the piles in order of use, starting clockwise from the pile of meat strips.

Thus, you will have: meat; onions, pepper, scallions, celery; bamboo shoots, mushrooms, and spinach (or cabbage); soybean curd slices (or vermicelli).

On a separate tray, you will have: a measuring cup, a bowl, the ¼ cup of oil, the bottle of soy sauce, a small jar of sugar, the cup of strong bouillon, and a bottle of Sake, if obtainable. Sherry is an acceptable replacement.

Finally, as the guests look on hungrily, you start to prepare the Sukiyaki. First, heat the oil in the chafing dish; throw in the meat slices and brown quickly on all sides.

Combine the bouillon, soy sauce, sugar in the bowl, and add about half to the chafing dish. Push the meat to one side of the dish, and add: onions, scallions, celery, and green pepper.

Cook over low heat for 3 minutes. Add the remaining stock, the bamboo shoots, mushrooms and spinach (or cabbage). Again cook gently for 3 minutes. Finally add the bean curd slices (or the cooked vermicelli), and simmer for another 3 minutes. Add ½ cup of Sake (if you can get it—and if not, substitute a tablespoon of dry sherry), heat for a minute, stirring gently.

Serve immediately, on top of plain boiled rice.

RISOTTO and CHINESE FRIED RICE

This is the "other" way to prepare rice—and every country boasts some dish made this way. It is simply raw rice browned in fat, then cooked in meat juice . . . with innumerable variations. The best known is

Italian Risotto

1½ cups ordinary white rice	1 tsp salt
2 T olive oil	½ tsp pepper
2 (or more) cups chicken consomme or bouillon	

Heat olive oil in a large frying pan, add washed rice and stir until it turns a golden brown (about 5 minutes). Reduce heat and add a cup of consomme or bouillon. Stir briskly until bubbling stops; cover tightly and simmer over lowest heat for 5 minutes. Add more consomme, re-cover and continue to simmer.

Subsequently check the rice every 5 minutes or so, adding consomme as needed. Overall, the cooking should take about 25-30 minutes, to produce a tender brown-tinged rice that has absorbed all the liquid.

This is a basic recipe—but any gourmet chef can produce infinite variations, such as adding:

¼ cup grated Parmesan cheese

a clove of pressed garlic

¼ tsp each of basil and oregano

1 tsp of chervil, and ½ tsp celery salt

½ cup of any diced leftover meat, fish or chicken

Chinese Fried Rice

This differs from Risotto in that it uses cooked rice and contains an addition of some kind of vegetable or meat. . . .

2 T oil

1 cup coarsely chopped onion

1 cup cold cooked rice (or prepare a cup of quick-cooking rice at the start of the dish—to be ready when needed)

1 T soy sauce

½ tsp salt

2 slightly beaten eggs

1 cup of additions such as:
Minced cooked chicken, pork, beef, ham (or a leftover)
Minced shrimp, lobster or crab meat
½ cup minced green peppers
½ cup minced nuts: peanuts, almonds, hazelnuts, etc.

Heat the oil, saute onions until brown, add cooked rice (or quick-cooking as above), and saute the rice until it browns. Add eggs, soy sauce and salt, and the cup of "addition." Saute for a further five minutes.

CHAPTER 9

VEGETABLES

A gourmet can make a meal of vegetables alone—if properly cooked.

Vegetables must be slightly undercooked and firm.

A pressure cooker is excellent for artichokes, beets, turnips and such—but tricky for softer vegetables which may easily turn into a mush, since cooking times are only 2 or 3 minutes.

Gourmet cooks depend upon frozen vegetables—and upon steaming baskets which are expandable metal gadgets that fit into any average saucepan, and hold the vegetables over steaming hot water so that all the flavorful juice is retained.

The best sauce for any vegetable is plain melted butter with a seasoning of salt and pepper—but Hollandaise is the traditional gourmet dressing for asparagus, broccoli and artichokes.

As a general rule, the simpler the main dish, the fancier the sauce for the vegetable—and vice versa.

Thin slices of white onion enhance carrots, peas and all kinds of beans; crisp slivers of toasted almonds, hazelnuts or Macadamia nuts are delicious with Brussels sprouts, spinach and broccoli; a slight sprinkle of caraway seed is fun with noodles, and parsley goes with absolutely *everything*—if you like it.

Grated Parmesan cheese is a gourmet addition to any baked or broiled vegetable, such as zucchini, mushrooms or tomatoes.

Never overlook the possible goodies in your neighborhood! Many a fresh water spring is surrounded by watercress, free for your picking . . . and when it comes to food, a gourmet never misses a bet. Watercress is a wonderful salad; a delightful soup; it is beloved of all English tea parties—rolled up in thin-sliced, de-crusted bread and butter, and chilled into dainty cigarette-shaped sandwiches—but it's also a delicious vegetable.

CRESSON A LA CRÈME

2 pounds of watercress   4 tablespoons of butter
4 tablespoons of heavy cream   salt and pepper

Pick over the watercress, discarding tough stems and damaged leaves. Blanch in boiling water for 5 minutes, drain and rinse with cold water, pressing out as much as possible of the excess water.

Melt the butter in a saucepan, add the cress and season with salt and pepper to taste. Simmer slowly for about 10 minutes, stirring frequently until soft.

Just before serving, add the cream and reheat—but do not boil. Serve very hot.

BAKED ENDIVE

In many parts of the U.S., true Belgian endive is apparently almost unknown, and greengrocers will insist upon offering chicory in its place (and if you then, cunningly, ask for chicory, they look completely blank!). But real endive (which is pronounced "ahndeev," please!) is a delicious, smooth-leafed, white-shading-to-pale-lemon-colored salad vegetable, shaped rather like an extra special Corona Corona cigar. It can be bought in tins, if fresh endive is not available.

4 fine fat endives   ½ cup melted butter
4 thin slices boiled ham   ½ teaspoon ground nutmeg
4 hard-boiled eggs, shelled
  and cut in half

If you use fresh endive, boil in salted water for 10-12 minutes, or until tender. Drain thoroughly. Then wrap each endive in a slice of ham, place in a buttered baking dish and surround tastefully with the halved eggs. Pour the melted butter over the endive, sprinkle with nutmeg, and bake 10 minutes at 400.

NOTE: If you really cannot obtain endive either fresh or tinned, celery hearts can be substituted.

LITTLE FRENCH PEAS

2 boxes frozen "tiny" peas
1 heart of lettuce
12 small white onions (or large drained tin)
4 tablespoons butter

1 teaspoon sugar
1 tablespoon minced fresh parsley
1 teaspoon chervil
½ teaspoon salt

Melt butter in a heavy saucepan, add the peas (slightly defrosted, if possible), the peeled onions and the lettuce heart cut in shreds. Sprinkle parsley, chervil, sugar and salt over the peas, stir thoroughly until the butter is well distributed over the peas. Then add 4 tablespoons of cold water, bring to a boil, cover tightly and reduce heat to a minimum. Cook for 15 minutes, add another 2 tablespoons of butter and serve at once.

CARROTS FLAMANDE

12 small scraped carrots, or
1 tin tiny whole carrots
3 tablespoons butter
1 teaspoon salt

1 teaspoon sugar
¼ teaspoon pepper
¼ cup heavy sweet cream

Melt butter, add carrots and seasonings, cover and cook over the lowest heat for 15 minutes or until carrots are tender. Add the cream, stir thoroughly and simmer 4 minutes.

CURRIED SPINACH

1 box frozen spinach
3 T butter
½ tsp dry mustard

1 tsp curry powder
¼ tsp paprika
½ tsp salt

Cook the spinach and drain thoroughly; melt butter and seasonings in a frying pan. Add the spinach and coat well with the curry-butter mixture.

A box of frozen zucchini can be used instead of spinach.

100

RATATOUILLE (ra-ta-tooy)

A home-style French vegetable casserole—a good dish for Sunday night supper.

2 cloves of garlic
4 T olive oil
2 large onions, thinly sliced
2 green (or sweet red) peppers, seeded and sliced

1 small eggplant, sliced ¼ inch thick
2 small zucchini, thinly sliced
3 small tomatoes, thinly sliced

Heat olive oil, add thinly sliced garlic cloves and onions. Saute 8 minutes. Add green or red peppers, eggplant and zucchini, and saute very gently for 8 minutes; add the tomatoes, stir very gently to move the vegetables into different positions for the final cooking. Cover tightly and simmer for 10 minutes.

For a substantial one-dish meal, a couple of small cold boiled potatoes can be added in thin slices together with the onions, or the vegetable stew can be served with plain boiled rice . . . in either case, each portion should be topped with a poached or fried egg.

AMERICAN RATATOUILLE

1 box frozen okra, cooked and drained
1 large green pepper, seeded and thinly sliced
2 onions, thin sliced
½ cup sliced celery
2 tomatoes, peeled and quar-

tered (1 large drained tin of tomatoes)
1 clove of garlic, sliced very thinly
1½ cups of white sauce
4 poached eggs

Cook and drain the okra.

Steam green pepper, onions and celery while okra cooks.

Make the white sauce from a tin of condensed cream of celery soup combined with 1 cup thin cream.

Combine all the vegetables, plus the garlic, in a casserole; cover with the white sauce and simmer for 15 minutes.

Serve the vegetables on buttered toast or plain boiled rice, and top each portion with a poached egg.

ASPERGES PARMESANES

2 packages frozen asparagus, cooked and drained

½ cup Parmesan cheese grated

¼ cup melted butter

1 teaspoon nutmeg

Cook the asparagus until just underdone, and drain. Place in a buttered baking dish, sprinkle with grated cheese, melted butter and nutmeg, and place in the oven for 15 minutes.

HOLLANDAISE SAUCE

The traditional lemon-butter-egg sauce for vegetables can be bought in jars at any good food shop, and although expensive, it may prove cheaper in the long run—because Hollandaise is tricky to make.

It should be a smooth emulsion—but all too often it will curdle before your very eyes; it is very temperamental and must be prepared and served *at once* or it will grow tired of waiting and separate dispiritedly in the sauce boat.

All depends upon the cooking. Hollandaise should be prepared in the top of a double boiler . . . and in theory, the sauce is to be blended and warmed by gentle steaming. Thus, the water in the bottom part of your double boiler should be hot but never allowed to boil—and the amount of water should always be well below any possibility of contact with the double boiler top. Furthermore, the heavier the construction of the double boiler top—so that it does not heat up too rapidly—the less risk of failure. An old-fashioned earthenware mixing bowl (if you can arrange it to fit at the top of a saucepan), is excellent for Hollandaise.

Success or failure, Hollandaise takes only about 5 minutes to make—thus, it's wise to have everything else completed and ready to serve before you begin the sauce. Asparagus, broccoli, artichokes or whatever—all should be on their serving dishes, awaiting the final touch . . . and the *instant* the sauce is blended, you will be able to distribute it over the vegetables before it has a chance to separate.

The ingredients for Hollandaise:

¼ pound of butter, *very cold* and cut in three pieces

2 egg yolks

1 T lemon juice

¼ tsp salt

a dash of Cayenne pepper

Place the egg yolks and lemon juice in an unheated double boiler top, set over the hot water and add a piece of butter. Stir gently until it melts; immediately add the next piece of butter, and continue to stir until it is melted, add the final piece of butter, plus salt and pepper. Stir gently but constantly . . . and the instant the last bit of butter is melted and absorbed in the sauce—SERVE IT!

If the sauce insists upon curdling, add *heavy* cream or boiling water, drop by drop, stirring constantly until the emulsion is restored . . . and if it refuses to pull itself together after 2 tablespoons of cream or water, you must accept it as a total defeat.

A second method of preparing Hollandaise is slightly more foolproof, but does not produce quite such a handsome sauce.

Using the proportions above—

Cream the butter thoroughly in a heavy bowl, beat in the egg yolks and lemon juice gradually, and season. Set the bowl over hot water and stir constantly until the mixture thickens slightly—then remove from the hot water until you are about ready to use the Hollandaise.

At this final moment, add boiling water—1 teaspoon at a time—and stir constantly until the sauce is an acceptable consistency. You will need about 4 teaspoons of boiling water . . . but add them very slowly, and stop as soon as the sauce is the right thickness.

POTATOES

In gourmet cookery, potatoes are served sparingly—but deliciously. They are often replaced in menu-planning by: rice, noodles, spaghetti, green noodles, garlic bread, squab stuffing—or the grated Parmesan cheese topping for a broiled dish—because a gourmet cook concentrates on the well-

103

rounded meal, rather than merely a succession of rich foods.

For quick cookery, there are packaged potatoes, but unless carefully prepared, these are never worthy of inclusion in a gourmet meal.

Packaged mashed potatoes—if you use thin cream in place of water and a full quarter pound of melted butter—will be just-barely-acceptable as mashed potatoes . . . but they are fine for the basis of Potatoes Duchesse or Chantilly.

Frozen potato patties are not nearly so good as Zurich potatoes; frozen stuffed baked potatoes are acceptable with ordinary meals, but far short of a gourmet effort, due to the excessive amount of cheap seasoning used by packagers.

And definitely, frozen French Fries will never approximate the start-from-scratch variety for gourmet standards. Fortunately, home-made authentic French fried potatoes are not difficult to prepare . . . even when you are keeping an eye on a Chateaubriand!

FRENCH FRIED POTATOES

The underlying theory of perfect French Fries is to dunk *cold* potato slices into very *hot* fat, and after they are browned, to drain them completely of every drop of cooking fat and serve quickly. Idaho potatoes are best for French Fries because they can be cut in the distinguished long slim sticks—but any other kind of potato can also be used, from Maine to Long Island to what's in your own garden.

1 peeled medium-sized Idaho potato per serving portion
A frying kettle, equipped with deep frying fat and a frying basket
Salt

First, peel potatoes, cut in sticks about ½ inch per side, and place in *cold* water.

Heat the frying fat; if you possess an electric frying kettle, follow the directions for your particular brand. If you are using the aluminum-saucepan-plus-strainer arrangement, use a thermometer and heat fat to 350.

Drain the potato slices on a linen or paper towel, patting

104

each individual stick dry. Distribute in the frying basket neatly, so that all the potatoes will be submerged in the first plunge . . . then lower frying basket into hot fat, gently. Be sure the first rolling boil of frying fat will not bubble up and over the side of the kettle, where it may possibly catch fire from the gas flame! Once sitting in the hot fat, you may forget the potatoes for about 10 minutes; then redistribute the browned bottom sticks by vigorous shaking of the fry-basket, and return to the hot fat for a final 10 minutes, or until all potatoes are golden brown. Now turn off the heat and drain the fry-basket; shake it occasionally to hasten draining of excess fat—and plan to serve within 5 minutes.

Never try to keep French Fried potatoes warm for more than 5 minutes before serving; they become sad and limp if placed in an oven and will end by being no better than the bought frozen packages. The end-result of French frying, is to produce a food that is cooked and soft within, but crisp and hot without. Anything less than this may be edible, but can only be considered as a failure by the cook.

FRENCH FRIED ONIONS

These, too, can be bought either frozen or in cans (which are good on a canape tray)—but it is not difficult to make your own and the difference will be tremendous.

2 eggs, slightly beaten
½ cup of milk
Seasoned flour (2 cups, with salt, pepper and paprika)

Onions: 2 or 3, depending on the size

Bermuda or Spanish onions are excellent for French frying, but the ordinary yellow or white, and the sweet red Italian varieties are equally serviceable.

Peel the onions and cut into ½ to ¾ inch slices; separate each slice into rings. Combine beaten egg and milk, and soak onions while heating the fat kettle to 350. Drain the onion rings a few at a time and drop into a deep bowl containing seasoned flour. Toss until thoroughly coated, then carefully transfer to frying basket, layering the onions so all of them will be submerged at the first plunge into the hot fat.

Finally, give the basket one good *shake*—to remove any excess flour—and place in the hot frying fat. After ten minutes, redistribute the onion rings individually, if necessary to get a better coloring on the top rings—but do not redistribute by shaking as with French Fried Potatoes or you will dislocate the crisp crust about the rings. When all are delicately browned, drain thoroughly for 5 minutes and serve at once.

ZURICH POTATOES

Crispy browned on the bottom, and soft white potato on top. This is a quick dish that practically cooks itself while you are busy with other matters.

3 or 4 Idaho potatoes, peeled	2 T each fresh minced parsley and green pepper
½ cup butter	
1 small white onion, grated	Paprika

Peel potatoes and grate them on the coarsest grater slot, placing them in cold water. Let stand for 5 minutes, then drain by handfuls, squeezing out all the milky potato starch. Dry on clean toweling. Melt half the butter in a large skillet, add grated onion and pepper, and saute 2 minutes. Add the drained dry potatoes. Sprinkle thickly with paprika, cover tightly and cook over a very low flame for 15 minutes. Check occasionally to be sure the potatoes are not sticking to the bottom of the pan—but do not stir or disarrange! Merely lift up with a spatula and add the rest of the butter if needed. Continue to cook for another 10 minutes.

POTATOES DUCHESSE, CHANTILLY, ANNA, NOISETTES

Four traditional French preparations for potatoes.

Potatoes Duchesse

2 cups of mashed potatoes— HOT	¼ tsp nutmeg
2 whole eggs	2 T melted butter
2 egg yolks	1 tsp salt
	¼ tsp black pepper

Add the butter and seasonings to the hot mashed potato; add the eggs and egg yolks, and beat the potato mixture until fluffy.

NOTE: These are the mashed potatoes used for rosettes in pastry tube garnish. In quick cookery, you won't have time for this, but you can serve Duchesse Potatoes by plain tablespoons, to accompany the finest steaks or chops.

Potatoes Chantilly

2 cups mashed potato	¼ cup grated Parmesan cheese
¼ cup heavy cream, *whipped*	

Place the mashed potato in a greased baking dish, just large enough to make four deep portions.

Whip the cream very stiff and distribute over the mashed potato; sprinkle with the grated cheese, and bake in a 475 oven until the cheese melts and the top is golden brown-bubbly.

Potatoes Anna

Take more than 30 minutes to bake, but they are so stand-ard in gourmet cookery that the recipe cannot be omitted.

3 or 4 potatoes, depending on size

3 small white onions, peeled and grated

½ pound melted butter— mixed with:

1 tsp chervil, 1 T minced fresh parsley, ½ tsp tar-ragon, ½ tsp paprika, 1 tsp salt, ¼ tsp black pepper

Heat the oven to 450.

Peel potatoes and thin-slice on the large slot of a grater, placing the potatoes in cold water.

Combine butter and herbs in a pipkin, to melt gently over low heat.

Butter a casserole *very* generously.

Drain potato slices; line the casserole dish with overlap-ping sections on bottom and side. Arrange them artistically because traditionally this is a dish that should be unmolded.

Sprinkle some of the grated onion and butter mixture over the bottom layer; add more potato slices, more onion and butter—and so on to the top.

Sprinkle the top thickly with paprika and minced parsley, and bake in a hot (475) oven for 20 minutes. Reduce heat to 400 and continue to bake a further 20 minutes, or until potatoes are soft and cooked through.

Unmold on a serving dish, to be portioned at table.

Potatoes Noisette

Potatoes Noisette are simply tiny potato balls, oven-browned in butter . . . and probably easiest of all: Drain one or two tins of small Irish potatoes (depending on how many potato balls you want); place in a shallow baking pan with ¼ cup of butter, sprinkle with 2 T minced parsley, and brown in a moderate oven for about 20-25 minutes. Turn the potatoes over, once in a while, to brown all sides.

CHAPTER 10

THE LAST RESORT: EGGS

Eggs are universal, ubiquitous and unreplaceable.

Eggs can be used for any meal at all—they can be simple and filling, or chichi and spiced . . . and they are one of the foods that is highly *personal.*

Everyone has his own taste in eggs. Gourmet egg cookery is not easy, therefore, because some like their eggs well-done and others like 'em raw . . .

Every country in the world has its own method of preparing and serving eggs . . . and the quick-cooking preparations are largely in the West. In Eastern countries there are:

EGYPTIAN EGGS (Hamine)

Place eggs in a saucepan of cold water, together with the brown outside skins of several onions. Boil the eggs gently for 2 hours or longer. The onion skins turn both the egg shells and egg whites a delicate brown.

ISTANBUL EGGS

Place eggs in a saucepan, cover with olive oil, Turkish coffee and the brown skins of 3 large onions. Cover the pan and simmer very very gently for a minimum of 12 hours.

CHINESE EGGS

4 eggs	2 T soy sauce
2 T butter	

Boil the eggs for 7 minutes, plunge in cold water, and shell. Melt butter in a saucepan, adding soy sauce and eggs, and cook gently for 5 minutes, basting and turning all the time until the eggs become dark brown.

These are served cold in slices.

ARABIAN EGGS

4 hardboiled eggs—shelled and still warm	½ tsp salt
4 T butter	½ tsp each: paprika, pepper, cinnamon—mixed together

Melt the butter. Prick the egg whites all over with a fork, then add the eggs to the butter and turn over and over, so the butter can soak into the egg. Cook until light brown, place on a warmed serving dish and sprinkle with the salt and spices.

SWISS EGGS

¼ lb imported Gruyere cheese (sliced thin)	1 tsp salt
4 eggs	½ tsp pepper
¼ cup heavy cream	butter
	grated cheese

Butter a shallow casserole, line with thin cheese slices. Break the eggs neatly into the casserole, keeping them whole. Add salt and pepper to cream, and pour over the eggs. Top with grated cheese and bake 10 minutes in a moderate oven.

Brown the cheese topping under the broiler for a few minutes, if necessary.

PIPERADE

The Basque version of our Texas or Western omelets.

2 green peppers	1 large chopped yellow onion
2 tomatoes, peeled and quartered	1 clove of garlic, pressed
2 T olive oil	4 eggs
	salt and pepper, to taste

Heat the oil, add chopped onion and sliced pepper; saute gently for 10 minutes. Add tomatoes and garlic, salt and pepper, and simmer until reduced to a soft mush, stirring and crushing occasionally with a fork. Add 4 slightly beaten eggs, stir constantly until eggs are set. Serve on buttered toast or thin slices of fried ham—or just plain. It's good any way you serve it.

CREOLE EGGS

A Sunday night supper dish—serve with plain boiled rice.
8 hardboiled eggs, shelled and sliced

Creole sauce

1 tin condensed cream of celery soup
½ cup milk
¾ cup drained canned tomatoes
1 T minced parsley

1 small onion, sliced thin
½ small green pepper, seeded and chopped
1 clove of garlic
2 T butter

Saute onion, pepper and minced garlic in butter for 5 minutes, while preparing the Creole sauce. Combine sauce and vegetables. Distribute a few tablespoons of the sauce over the bottom of a buttered casserole, top with some of the hardboiled eggs, and make alternate layers of sauce and egg slices. End with a layer of sauce, sprinkle thickly with bread crumbs and grated Parmesan cheese, and bake 20 minutes in a 375 oven.

SCRAMBLED EGGS A L'INDIENNE

1 large tart eating apple, diced
2 onions, chopped
3 T butter

4 eggs
¼ cup tomato sauce
½ tsp curry powder

Saute onions and apple in butter until soft—about 10 minutes.
Add curry powder and stir well.
Beat eggs slightly, add the tomato sauce and blend.
Combine with the apple-onion mixture and cook gently over low heat, stirring occasionally until eggs are set and cooked soft.

111

EGGS BENEDICT and EGGS FLORENTINE

These are the great poached egg dishes, to serve for brunch, Sunday supper or unexpected guests. An egg poacher makes them quick to prepare.

Eggs Benedict

4 English muffins, split, toasted and buttered

8 pieces of ham or Canadian bacon, sauteed in butter

8 poached eggs

8 T Hollandaise sauce (½ cup)

Warm the prepared Hollandaise sauce in a double boiler —to make Eggs Benedict in 30 minutes really will be easier with store-bought sauce!

Saute ham or Canadian bacon gently in 2 tablespoons of butter.

Split, and butter the English muffins; toast in the broiler (an electric broiler is helpful, here). When lightly browned, remove and keep warm.

Poach the eggs—2 eggs for each portion, so even a 4-position egg poacher will require two operations.

Top each muffin half with a bit of ham or cooked Canadian bacon; place a poached egg atop the meat. Finally, dribble a tablespoon of warm Hollandaise sauce over each egg, and serve.

EGGS FLORENTINE

Anything "Florentine" indicates a base of spinach—and this dish is, quite simply, poached eggs on a bed of cooked spinach, topped by Mornay sauce—which is a rich cheese cream sauce.

2 boxes frozen chopped spinach, cooked and well-drained

8 poached eggs

1 cup sauce Mornay

2 T grated Parmesan cheese

Steam-cook the chopped spinach while you prepare the sauce (see below).

112

Heat the broiler oven, and start poaching the eggs.

Drain the spinach and place in a buttered casserole dish; top with the poached eggs. Cover thickly with the warm sauce and sprinkle with cheese.

Broil for a few minutes until the top browns.

MORNAY SAUCE

This is a variation of Bechamel sauce, which is a fussy French version of plain old white sauce. A quick approximation of sauce Mornay—

½ tin condensed mushroom soup	1 egg yolk
an equal amount of thin cream	2 T grated Parmesan
	1 T butter

Combine soup and cream, blend well and strain through a fine sieve to remove mushroom bits. Warm in a double boiler, add slightly beaten egg yolk, and stir well. Add cheese and butter, and stir until completely melted.

SOUFFLÉS

A souffle is viewed with reverence and awe, because *everyone* has heard that this is A Production. Myths abound when it comes to souffles; they are supposedly incredibly fussy to prepare . . . difficult to cook . . . and inclined to wilt despondently unless rushed on roller skates from oven to table.

None of these things is true, especially today. *Anyone* can make a delicious main dish souffle, produce it to the applause of the diners and acquire a fine reputation for gourmet cookery!

Strictly speaking, souffles are out of bounds for a 30-minute gourmet chef, because despite the electric egg beater and substituting condensed cream soup for the fussy white sauce base of yesterday's souffle recipes, there is still no way to shorten the baking time. Inevitably this consumes an absolute minimum of half an hour in the oven (if you can bear the French type of souffle which is supposed to be moist,

113

even a bit liquid in the center). For a proper souffle (that is, to our personal taste), you must allow 45 minutes.

Still, we include the basic souffle recipe in this book . . . first, because it does not take more than 15 minutes *preparation* time, even though it needs another 45 minutes in the oven, and secondly, because everyone should be encouraged to try making souffles.

BASIC SOUFFLE RECIPE

1 can condensed cream soup, thin with ½ cup cream
4 eggs, separated, plus an extra egg white

1 cup of diced meat, chicken, fish, shredded cheese—or what you wish

Heat the oven to 375.

Heat soup in a double boiler top while separating the eggs. (If you are making a cheese souffle, melt the cheese with the soup.)

Beat the egg yolks until thick and lemon-colored.

Beat the egg whites separately until *very* stiff.

Remove the soup pot and add egg yolks, stirring well. Add meat, fish, vegetables, chicken or anything but cheese at this point. Butter a casserole dish very generously, while the soup mixture cools slightly. Then fold in the stiff egg whites, gently turn the batter into the dish and bake for 30 minutes, or more.

There are things to know about a souffle. First, a souffle is an utterly simple matter of enriching a basic white sauce with beaten egg yolks, then capturing all the air possible through gently folding in stiff-beaten egg whites, which automatically expand in oven heat and carry the rest of the mixture onward and upward.

Secondly, it is true that a souffle does not like to be kept waiting; far better, on souffle night, to collect the diners at table to finish their cocktails and let them wait for the souffle!

Thirdly, a souffle casserole may be set in a pan of warm water in the oven and baked in the same way as a baked custard . . . and if you choose this method, there will be no crust on bottom or sides. Other chefs advise baking a main dish souffle in an unbuttered casserole, so the batter will cling to the sides, form a seal, and force the expanding air even farther upward. A smaller group quietly adds a tablespoon of brandy during the final folding operation, because the spirits not only aid in quick-setting the egg batter but add their own expanding fumes to create the desired puffy brown top.

An extra egg white is additional insurance for a high-minded soufflé.

CHAPTER 11

BREADSTUFF:

There is practically nothing to be added to the bewildering and delicious varieties of breads, rolls, and crackers available in any corner grocery. Despite the national preoccupation with our waistlines, we are certainly the most versatile country with starches!

What's needed for a gourmet chef today is simply a spirit of adventure, and some concept of what goes best with what. . . .

Crusty French and Italian bread goes with French, Italian and Spanish dishes—and is also best with any kind of salad

Pumpernickel and thin-sliced rye is better with Scandinavian, German and Russian foods.

The farther East one goes, the less the bread—as such. Matzos and thin wheat crackers can approximate the unleavened breads of the Near East and the chupatties of India —but in the true Oriental menu, rice replaces bread.

Aside from "brown and serve" packages, almost all homemade breads take more than 30 minutes to prepare—but in case you have a few extra minutes, some do-it-yourself recipes are included here. It would be a pity to miss such distinctively American items as HUSH PUPPIES and SPOON BREAD . . .

HUSH PUPPIES

These are supposedly an invention of the camp cooks during the Western expansion of pioneer days, when leftover cornmeal dough was fried and thrown to the camp dogs. Who knows if this is true—but if so, one can only envy those dogs!

2 cups yellow corn meal	⅔ cup milk
2 tsp baking powder	1 egg
1 tsp salt	Hot bacon fat, for frying
1 large onion, finely chopped	

Mix corn meal, baking powder, salt and onion; add milk and egg to form a *stiff* mixture.

Heat a shallow frying pan of bacon fat—and if you can combine hush puppies with a meal in which you've fried fresh-caught trout in that bacon fat, you are a real gourmet cook!

Mold the hush puppies into rolls about half the size of a cigar—and fry until well-browned on all sides. Serve hot—with crisp-fried fish.

SPOON BREAD A *Southern States dish*

It is served on the dinner plate, replacing potatoes, and is eaten with a fork (and plenty of extra butter on top).

3 generous cups of milk	1 tsp salt
1½ cups *white* corn meal	2 T melted butter
3 well beaten eggs	1¾ tsp baking powder

Combine milk and corn meal, bring to a boil, making a mush, and remove from the fire.

Add eggs, salt, melted butter and baking powder and mix well. Place in a greased casserole in a medium oven for 35-45 minutes, or until a knife inserted in the middle of the dish comes out clean.

Much of what is sold as French or Italian bread is regrettably less than gourmet-standards. Encased in germ-proof wrappings, it is sometimes more limp than "crusty," and will require 5 minutes in a warm oven before worthy of appearance at table.

Dispirited French and Italian bread can be revived as "herbed bread," also. Spread leftover slices with any of the herb butters listed below, place on a shallow baking pan and brown—either in the oven or beneath the broiler. Limp or hardened loaves can also be cut diagonally nearly to the

117

bottom, spread with herb butters and rejuvenated in the ho
oven . . . but know your own stove, for the bread ma
crisp to burning point more rapidly than you expect!

HERB BUTTERS

Cream a quarter pound of butter with any of the following

1. 2 cloves of garlic, pressed
2. 4 T each fresh parsley and chives, minced
3. 4 T fresh minced parsley and 1 T crumbled thyme
4. 2 T crumbled tarragon with 4 T fresh chopped chive
5. 1 T powdered marjoram, and 2 T fresh minced parsle
6. 1 T each of powdered sage and summer savory, with ƙ
   T minced fresh parsley

Leftover bread slices spread with any of the herb butter
can also be enhanced by a sprinkling of grated Parmesar
cheese.

The great basic French and Italian bread accompaniments
are Parmesan and Garlic bread—and these add the extra
gourmet touch to a Sunday night supper of Chef's Salad or
omelette, as well as being indispensable for all winter-night
soups.

Both are a simple matter of spreading leftover sliced
French or Italian bread with butter and browning briefly beneath the broiler—but there are differences:

PARMESAN TOAST: spread bread slices with soft butter
and sprinkle thickly with grated Parmesan cheese. Brown
lightly.

GARLIC BREAD: cream butter with 1 (or 2, depending
on the amount you are making) pressed cloves of garlic.
Spread on bread and brown lightly.

BASIC MUFFINS

These are simple enough to make for a Sunday night supper or special brunch . . . and are capable of infinite variations!

1 cup flour	¼ cup milk
¼ tsp salt	1 T melted butter
2 tsp baking powder	2 T sugar
1 egg	

Heat the oven to 425.
Melt the butter.
Beat the egg, add salt, sugar, butter, part of the flour and the baking powder, mixing lightly and quickly. Add remaining flour and the milk, and stir until smooth. Fill greased muffin pan about half-full, and bake for 20 minutes in the oven.

Variations:

½ cup corn meal and ½ cup white flour
½ cup graham flour and ½ cup white flour

Additions:

¼ cup blueberries, fresh
½ cup finely chopped walnuts

CHAPTER 12

THE GOOD GREEN SALAD

Salads are vital to a gourmet meal.

They are not only delicious to eat, and hailed with delight by anyone on a diet, but they have a particular purpose and should be served at a particular moment: *after* the entree.

In these days of informal service, it is quite correct to serve the salad with the main dish—or to plan a good green salad in place of a vegetable to accompany the entree—but for a proper gourmet meal, a salad there must be, and it is to be eaten after the main course, in order to clear the palate in preparation for dessert and coffee.

While many Western states present the salad before anything else (including a shrimp or lobster cocktail), the knowledgeable gourmet quietly removes the salad plate to one side where it will await its proper mission in life.

In formal dinner service, the salad is served as a separate course . . . and you will note that all wine glasses for preceding courses are removed at the same time as the entree dishes. At a proper gourmet dinner, it will be too bad for you if you didn't finish the Chambertin with the Chateaubriand; the half-full glass will be firmly removed with the empty steak plate!

No wine is *ever* served with a salad course . . . because they are mutually exclusive to a gourmet. Both are used to sharpen the tastebuds—but to your palate wine does not mix with olive oil any better than it mixes with water.

THE GOOD GREEN TOSSED SALAD

The tossed green salad, to a gourmet, resembles the "little black dress" to a Best-Dressed Woman. It is absolutely correct for all meals; it can be dressed up or stand *au naturel,* and it will never be wrong as an accompaniment to any

120

meal . . . although it can be just as dull as one little black dress until you learn a few combinations and permutations.

The memorable salad depends upon its greens—which must be crisp and fresh, and daringly combined—and its dressing.

The gourmet cook devotes a special wooden bowl to salad-mixing. It is never soaked nor too-thoroughly washed. Wipe out with paper toweling, rinse with very hot water . . . just enough to remove any surface oil that might grow rancid . . . and wipe completely dry with plenty of paper toweling. A salad bowl seasons with the oil that soaks *into* the wood; all that should be removed after each using is the temporary detritus of coddled egg or anchovy bit, and unabsorbed oil.

For those who love garlic, rub a cut clove directly about the bowl each time you use it . . . or rub the garlic clove on cubes of stale French bread and toss with the salad. These are known as *chapons* (not to be confused with *croutons,* which are *fried* bits of bread).

There is a theory that salad greens should be torn apart rather than cut with a knife . . . and that if a knife is used, it should always be silver. We do not personally hold with this—because hand-torn greens are usually untidy to eat. In our kitchen, we dare to wash our greens, select only the tender inner bits, and cut them into fork-sized pieces with a common paring knife.

Nor has any guest so far protested the result . . .

The amount of greens to be used for a salad serving four people cannot be exactly specified: it will depend upon how well the diners like salad, how large the heads of lettuce, etc., and how many other dishes comprise the meal. In general, if you use a green salad to replace a vegetable or to accompany an entree of spaghetti or baked beans, it's wise to make lots of salad; if the main dish is simple and flanked by vegetables, less greens are needed. Something also depends upon the size of salad bowl or plate; half-filled will be easier to eat—and prepare for second helpings with the spaghetti-type of meal.

A green salad can be made of almost anything—and the

more combinations you learn, the better your gourmet reputation.

SALAD GREENS are far more varied than you may have supposed . . . and a fair selection of them will be available in any supermarket, although as usual, the people who live in the country will have the best of it.

Lettuce: Simpson, Iceberg, Romaine, Boston, curly red tinged Western lettuces.

Other Greens: Belgian endive, chicory, escarole, water cress, and spinach . . . some or all of these are generally available.

Specialties: Sorrel, field salad, dandelions, chard and beet tops, garden lettuce, tiny nasturtium leaves. Occasionally some of these appear, expensively, in the finest gourmet greengroceries of large cities—but on the whole, they can only be had when you have access to a kitchen garden. And if you do—what a salad reputation you can build!

The "good green salad" may also include vegetables: cabbage (red, white or Chinese), radishes, cucumbers, celery, raw carrots, tomatoes, scallions, *thin-sliced* white onion rings, avocado or hearts of palm.

Finally, there are the salad herbs, which if fresh may be sprinkled over the salad, or may be incorporated in the dressing if you only have dried herbs. Tarragon, chives, shallots, parsley, chervil, garlic.

Gourmets speak a snob-language of their own. Thus, one "builds" a salad, and "dresses" it—with oil, vinegar, mayonnaise or whatever.

To build a gourmet salad, emphasize greens first; use at least three if there are no vegetable additions. Thoroughly wash the greens and drain in a salad basket. For a major effect, use only the inner leaves and hearts of salad greens. After draining, cut into suitable pieces, pile loosely in a bowl and place in the refrigerator.

Salad dressing is always added at the last moment, preferably at table. Turn-toss the salad so that every leaf is coated with the dressing.

122

It is quite true that a salad is *built;* here's how . . .

Place chilled washed greens in the bottom of the salad serving bowl. Add ingredients in the following order, and stop when you choose.

Very thinly sliced white onion rings, separated . . . next a layer of raw carrot ribbons (use the commercial vegetable peeler) . . . quartered or sliced tomatoes . . . sliced green pepper rounds . . . coarsely cut hardboiled egg . . . fresh-minced parsley . . . coarsely cut Bleu cheese (or Gorgonzola, or Roquefort): any or all of these make a salad, garnished with crisp radishes, scallions, raw carrot sticks and cucumber wedges.

The less greens, the more vegetables—and vice versa—but pile the dish lightly and loosely, whatever you use, and bring it to the dinner table for the final preparation of salad dressing.

The ultimate gourmet presentation of salad, of course, is the ability to dress it freehand before the admiring eyes of your guests—and this is not too difficult, provided you have a steady hand and a little sense of rhythm.

There is only one vital point to a French dressing: it is *always* one part vinegar to three parts oil. All you have to do is use the same measure—and this may be the silver salad mixing spoon, or one tilt of the vinegar bottle to three tilts of the oil! After the critical oil-vinegar operation, add a teaspoon of salt (about 4 casual shakes of a small saltcellar) and ½ a teaspoon of pepper (or 4 generous twists of the pepper mill).

Then—mix your salad and serve it up with confidence.

Naturally, it is much simpler to dress a salad with a previously-prepared dressing, which you have made at leisure and to which you have given full concentration. A gourmet cook usually makes salad dressings by the quart, in several "flavors," and stores them at the bottom of the refrigerator (to be well shaken before using).

The best known salad dressings are French (Vinaigrette) and Mayonnaise—and it is possible that Shakespeare may have been thinking of them rather than Cleopatra when he wrote "Age cannot wither, nor custom stale, her infinite variety. . . ." for a real gourmet cook can do *anything* with either or a combination of both.

The tomato-colored sauce sold as French Dressing is *not*, only the 1-to-3 olive oil and vinegar preparation is authentic Commercial Mayonnaise, however, is regulated by law, and only a true egg-oil emulsion can be sold as mayonnaise dressing.

Other bottled dressings for salads exist in bewildering variety; some are acceptable and all are rather expensive in comparison to making your own, but for emergencies your best bet are the seasoning packets to be added quickly to olive oil and vinegar in a calibrated bottle.

BASIC FRENCH (VINAIGRETTE) DRESSING

This is also used for French hors d'oeuvres, particularly the vegetable salads, or to marinate celery root, etc.

1 cup vinegar: wine, tarra-gon or malt	2 tsp salt
3 cups good olive oil	1 tsp pepper

Place in a quart jar with a tight cap, and shake vigorously to blend. To this may be added any of the following variations:

1. 2 peeled sliced cloves of garlic
2. 2 T minced parsley, 3 minced shallots, 2 minced garlic cloves
3. 1 T minced chives, 1 T curry powder (use malt vinegar)
4. 2 T caraway seeds, 6 boned mashed sardines (use tarragon vinegar—for fish salads)
5. ½ cup minced pitted black olives
   4 minced gherkins
   2 mashed hardboiled egg yolks
   2 T minced parsley
   1 T drained chopped capers
   1 T fresh chopped chives
   (Use wine vinegar—and try this for vegetables or meat salads)

6. 1 T dry English mustard
   1 T Bahamian mustard
   2 T Worcestershire Sauce
   (Mix very smoothly together, taking out all lumps, and
   add to malt vinegar Vinaigrette—a sturdy basic
   dressing, excellent for Chef's salad)

7. ½ pound of Roquefort cheese, mashed with ¼ cup port
   wine
   1 T Bahamian mustard
   3 chopped scallions
   1 T each: Worcestershire and paprika
   2 minced cloves of garlic
   (Use with tarragon vinegar basic dressing—for plain
   green salads only)

8. 1 cup basic French dressing made with wine vinegar
   2 cups of mayonnaise
   3 chopped hardboiled eggs
   1 cup chili sauce
   1 T drained capers
   1 T minced sweet gherkins
   2 T heavy cream
   (Mix smoothly together: French dressing, mayonnaise
   and cream—and other ingredients. This is excellent
   for shrimps)

MAYONNAISE

While this can be readily bought in any shop, many
gourmet chefs prefer to make their own mayonnaise. Here's
how:

2 egg yolks	½ tsp dry mustard
½ tsp salt	2 tsp vinegar
¼ tsp white pepper	1 cup olive oil

Start with a bowl heated by rinsing in *very* hot water,
then thoroughly dried.

Beat the egg yolks with an electric beater, add pepper,
salt and mustard, and a teaspoon of vinegar. Mix well.

Add the olive oil—drop by drop at first, until about ¼ cup has been added. Put in ½ tsp more vinegar, continue to beat, and then add the rest of the oil in a slow trickle. Check occasionally to be sure the mayonnaise is combining smoothly. When all the oil has been added and absorbed, add the remaining ½ tsp vinegar.

Lemon or lime juice can be used to replace the vinegar— and gives a completely different flavor to the mayonnaise.

Home-made mayonnaise is a matter of minutes in an electric blender—in which case, follow the directions for your particular blender.

AIOLI

This is *garlic* mayonnaise. It is used with French peasant and Spanish meals. It has an extremely rich strong flavor, and is usually served with very plain boiled fish or potato salad, either hot or cold. Aioli tastes best when the garlic is crushed with mortar and pestle, but an approximation is possible with pressed garlic . . . particularly if you have the patience to put it through the garlic press a second time.

1 cup mayonnaise (homemade—if possible)
4 garlic cloves, peeled and pounded to smooth pulp in a mortar

Blend mayonnaise and garlic pulp until it is creamy-smooth.

AVOCADO DRESSING

Peel and halve 2 ripe avocados, place in a lettuce nest, and fill each avocado half with the following:

1 T olive oil	¼ tsp salt
1 tsp cold strong black coffee	1 generous sprinkle of black
1 pinch sweet basil	pepper
⅛ tsp sugar	

126

CHEF'S SALAD

Next in popularity to the green tossed salad, it is used as a main dish. Serve it with lots of hot garlic bread.

Traditionally a chef's salad contains equal amounts of chicken, tongue, ham and swiss cheese, cut in julienne strips and arranged in separate mounds on a bed of lettuce. The dish is decorated with sprigs of water cress, a quartered hardboiled egg and quartered peeled ripe tomato for each portion—plus a few olives and possibly some parsley.

It is always served separately from its dressing, which is Vinaigrette. In restaurant service, a Chef's Salad is served individually—but for home consumption, it is equally delicious to present it attractively in a family-sized bowl, to pour over the dressing with fancy abandon, and mix well before serving on separate plates.

Practically speaking, the Chef's Salad usually means "Whatever is in the refrigerator, garnished with hardboiled eggs and olives, and disguised by plenty of salad dressing!" But there is nothing wrong with this, and thus a *Chef's Salad Chez Vous* simply contains:

Cold cooked meats and chicken
Firm cheeses: American, Provolone, Swiss, Muenster, etc.
Lettuce: plenty of it; any kind
Garnishes: radishes, cucumbers, carrots, hardboiled eggs, etc.

A Chef's Salad depends entirely upon the *arrangement* of its components. Start with the salad greens, distribute the julienne piles of meats, chicken, cheese, separately over the top, garnish for eye appeal with the yellow-white eggs, red tomatoes or radishes, black olives.

CAESAR SALAD

Romaine lettuce, dressed with lemon juice instead of vinegar. One of the great traditional salads, it stands midway between the tossed green accompaniment salad and the main dish Chef's Salad.

2 cups croutons (garlic flavored)
2 heads romaine lettuce
¼ tsp dry mustard
¼ tsp black pepper
½ tsp salt
½ cup grated Parmesan cheese
6 T olive oil

juice of 2 lemons
2 coddled eggs
1 small drained tin of anchovy fillets, cut small (or 4 slices crumbled crisp-cooked bacon)
1 dash of Worcestershire (optional)
1 clove of garlic

Prepare the coddled eggs—1½ minutes in boiling water.

Rub the salad bowl with the cut garlic clove. Tear apart the chilled romaine lettuce into sensible-sized pieces. Sprinkle with mustard, pepper, salt and Parmesan cheese. Squeeze the two lemons directly over the salad (use a cocktail bar squeezer and watch out for any seeds that may elude you); add the oil, and Worcestershire.

Break the eggs over the greens, and toss thoroughly until all the egg has been absorbed.

Last of all, and just before serving, and cut anchovy fillets (or bacon bits), and the garlic-flavored croutons . . . it's usually wise to crisp the commercial croutons for a minute or two in a hot oven.

CRAB LOUIE

While no one seems certain who Louie was (and many cookbooks now dignify him with an s instead of an e), this is one of the great main dish salads. It may be served with shrimps or lobster in place of the crab meat—although one cannot know if this would meet with Louie's approval.

1½ pounds fresh crab meat (or three cans Geisha brand)
6 hardboiled eggs

2 tomatoes
black olives
Mayonnaise dressing—1½ cups

Pick over the crab meat (or drain and devein the canned crab). Mound on a bed of lettuce; dice the hardboiled eggs and sprinkle over crab meat. Top with the dressing, and garnish with tomato slices and black olives.

LOUIE'S DRESSING

1 cup mayonnaise
1 cup Vinaigrette (using tarragon vinegar)
3 cup chili sauce

1 teaspoon each Worcestershire and horseradish
1 T sweet pickle relish
½ tsp salt, ¼ tsp pepper

MUSHROOM SALAD

This goes with cold sliced chicken or tongue for a Sunday night supper.

1 pound fresh mushrooms
2 T fresh minced parsley

1 T fresh minced chives
Vinaigrette dressing

Wash and dry the mushroom caps (save the mushroom stems to use another day).

Slice the mushrooms thinly, and toss with parsley, chives, and Vinaigrette dressing prepared with wine vinegar (4 or 5 tablespoons of dressing—but use enough to coat the mushroom slices).

Chill and serve *very cold* on a lettuce leaf.

NOTE: This can also be used as part of a truce French hors d'oeuvres plate.

STUFFED AVOCADO SALAD

2 large ripe avocados, cut in half and pitted
¼ cup each, chopped green pepper, celery, grated carrot
1 small boiled potato, peeled and diced

1 T fresh chopped parsley
8 cooked shrimps, coarsely cut
1 tsp fresh chopped chives
2 scallions, chopped

Dressing:

2 T mayonnaise
2 T olive oil
2 hardboiled eggs, chopped

1½ tsp curry powder
1 clove pressed garlic (or ⅛ tsp garlic powder)

129

Mix the dressing smoothly, combine with other ingredients, and stuff into the avocados.

SHRIMP SALAD

Combine ½ cup mayonnaise with ½ cup plain French dressing. Add 2 tablespoons each chopped capers, gherkins, fresh parsley and 1 T ketchup. Mix smooth, and mix with 2 pounds shelled chilled shrimp.

CHAPTER 13

GILDING THE LILY: DESSERTS

Because most everyone is trying to eat their cake and retain their waistlines, too, few people eat desserts these days . . . and for all but the most impressive occasions, the quick-cook can stop dead with the salad. Coffee and liqueurs will suffice to round off the carte du jour.

Still, it's a pity to overlook the seasonal goodies of fresh fruits, and today's commercial ice creams and sherbets possess few calories (being mostly full of substitutes like gelatine unless rigidly controlled by State food laws).

Just as the salad is intended to cleanse the gourmet's taste-buds, so the dessert course has a real reason for existence, and should not be ignored. We no longer have the sweet-tooth that delights in cloying rich desserts—but fresh fruits in wine, or plain ice cream with a touch of good liqueur really do restore a taste balance after the hearty main dish.

For the sake of our diets, a gourmet cook does not serve cakes or pies or steamed puddings with brandied hard sauce except on great holiday occasions . . . but again, all depends upon the menu as a whole, for if the main part of the meal is extremely simple and plain, without rich sauces, Crêpes Suzette will be the focal point of the dinner, toward which every other dish has tended.

Any gourmet cook knows a dozen different combinations of fresh seasonal fruits, to be served with red wine, white wine. sherry, a dash of brandy or rum, or any good liqueur that happens to be at hand. Defrosted frozen fruits are excellent for this sort of dessert.

Similarly, any sort of plain ice cream may be topped by fresh or defrosted frozen fruits, or fruits from a tin—or by a tablespoon of good liqueur. A standard combination is Crème de Cacao dribbled over coffee ice cream.

And although modern diners often say "No dessert, thank

you," it is a fact that many of the greatest desserts of traditional gastronomy are utterly simple, uncloying, and easy on the waistline!

POIRES HELENE

This is simply well-drained tinned pears placed on vanilla ice cream, and covered with warm chocolate sauce.

PÊCHE MELBA

Place half a peach atop vanilla ice cream and cover with a raspberry sauce (Escoffier's Sauce Melba).

STRAWBERRIES ROMANOFF (2-Step Cookery— but all on one evening)

Here is a fancy dessert to be easily finished at the last moment—after the main course dishes are removed, and while guests are chatting, and digesting, in anticipation of dessert.

1½ quarts fresh ripe hulled strawberries (or 3 defrosted frozen packages)	2 T sugar (or a little more, depending on ripeness of berries)
Juice of a lemon	1 cup heavy cream, whipped stiff
½ cup Cointreau	1 pint vanilla ice cream

Step #1:

Clean strawberries, and slice if large; cover with sugar and 2 T Cointreau. Chill.

Allow the ice cream to defrost slightly—put it in the bottom part of the refrigerator instead of the ice compartment.

Step #2:

With an electric beater, whip the cream stiff. In another bowl, slightly whip the vanilla ice cream; fold in the whipped cream, add lemon juice and remaining Cointreau and blend smooth.

132

Pour the whipped ice cream over strawberries in a pretty serving dish, and bring to the table at once.

MERINGUE GLACÉ

4 pairs of meringue shells (make these yourself, perhaps
—to use up the accumulation of egg whites!)
ice cream
fruit, or liqueur, or special sauce

Despite the fancy name, a meringue glacé is simple: flank a small serving of suitable ice cream with a pair of meringue shells, and dribble sauce on top.

The combination depends on your imagination; traditionally, fudge sauce is used on vanilla ice cream—but why not try a tablespoon of Cointreau over peach ice cream, or fresh strawberries over raspberry ice?

If you couple meringues with ice cream, and top by plain sweetened whipped cream—nothing else—it is a Meringue Chantilly.

MERINGUES take an hour to bake, but the recipe is included because you will have to do *something* with all those egg whites that accumulate from fancy French sauces.

2 egg whites	½ tsp vanilla or any desired
½ cup sugar	flavoring (almond, maple, etc.)

Beat egg whites until very stiff and dry; add the sugar slowly beating constantly until the mixture holds its shape. Add remaining sugar and flavoring and form into neat little mounds on a cooky sheet covered with waxed paper. The mixture spreads, so do not make the mounds too large!

Bake about 50 minutes in a *very* slow oven (250).

WARNING: this makes between 18 and 22 meringues . . . they can be eaten as cookies, but otherwise your family may grow very tired of Meringue Glacé, Meringue Chantilly, and so on!

ZABAGLIONE

Italian wine-custard which may be served by itself, either hot or cold—or may be used as a sauce for other desserts. French cooks call this *Sabayon.*

8 egg yolks
4 heaping tablespoons of va-   with ¼ tsp vanilla extract
   nilla sugar (or plain sugar   ¼ cup Marsala wine

Combine in a double boiler over a very hot fire, beating constantly with a rotary egg beater until the mixture thickens to the consistency of thick cream.

Serve hot, by itself . . . or poured over chilled drained fruits (peaches, apricots, Kadota figs) . . . or over crumbled stale cake (sponge, pound cake, or any cake from which icing has been removed).

If you make it the previous evening and chill overnight, serve with a garnish of sliced Maraschino cherries and a teaspoon of Kirsch, Courvoisier or Grand Marnier floating on top—or use it for

TIPSY PUDDING

Place stale cake crumbs in serving dishes and sprinkle with a tablespoon or two of sherry, or brandy, or suitable liqueur.

Cover with Zabaglione, and chill.

Decorate with Maraschino cherry bits, and a teaspoon of whatever liqueur was used on the stale cake.

DESSERT SOUFFLÉS

These are far simpler than the main dish variety, principally because the chef has a "captive audience" awaiting the masterpiece: guests are already at table while the soufflé bakes off-stage, and all that is required for a fabulous effect is a clever hostess, able to control conversation so the first courses are finished and cleared away within 25-30 minutes.

Unless you have an exceptionally voluble guest, you may

dare to produce either of the following as a superelegant garnish for even the humblest meal.

CHOCOLATE SOUFFLÉ

2 squares bitter chocolate   4 eggs, separated (plus an
2 T water   extra egg white)
3 T sugar

Melt chocolate, water and sugar in a double boiler until smooth. Remove from heat and add egg yolks one at a time, stirring very vigorously. Beat the egg whites very stiff, and fold into the chocolate mixture delicately. Finally, pile in a generously buttered baking dish, and place in the oven for 20-25 minutes at moderate (375) heat. Serve with whipped cream, flavored with dark rum.

If you like, you may also add 2 tablespoons of the dark Jamaica rum as you fold in the egg whites.

For this dish, do not skimp the butter on the casserole dish, as it is the butter that will set the mixture and force it upwards.

LEMON SOUFFLÉ

4 eggs, separated   ⅔ cup of sugar
1 lemon—grated rind and
    juice

Beat egg yolks until very thick, adding sugar gradually. Add lemon rind and juice. Beat egg whites very stiff; cut and fold into lemon mixtures, pour into a generously buttered soufflé dish, and bake 20-25 minutes in a moderate oven.

CHAFING DISH desserts are a boon to the quick gourmet cook: enormously impressive to guests and delightfully simple to create.

It is an odd fact that hungry people will happily wait for as much as an hour to dine . . . so long as they can see the food being prepared before them!

CHERRIES JUBILEE can be duplicated with any fruit you happen to have around—to dress up a meal of leftovers with the final fancy touch. Best of all, the dessert course can be forgotten until the last moment—provided you know what you are going to use for it.

2 cups Bing cherries	Vanilla ice cream for 4 servings
2 ounces of Kirsch (or good brandy)	

Heat cherries in their juice in the top of a chafing dish; add the Kirsch (or brandy), light with a match and stir until the flames die. Serve over vanilla ice cream.

Here is one of the great basic recipes which is capable of infinite permutations and combinations!

For all flaming fruits over ice cream, brandy is acceptable —but there will be an extra flavor if a fruit liqueur is also used. Fresh peaches in their juice, extended by peach brandy and flamed with 2 ounces of Armagnac, served over coffee ice cream—or defrosted packages of raspberries or strawberries, brandy-flamed and served with fresh peach ice cream. . . . Make up your own personal combinations, combining whatever is in the liqueur closet with a suitable fruit.

CRÊPES SUZETTE

Thin pancakes in a flaming liqueur sauce. This is Henri Charpentier's own recipe—and as he invented the dish in Monte Carlo in 1898 for HRH Edward, Prince of Wales, it is unquestionably definitive . . . but not impossible to recreate.

The real difficulty in making perfect crêpes Suzette is to make *tender* pancakes. The sauce should be made in advance, and allowed to mature. In fact, if you can master the art of the pancakes, you may dare to make the sauce in large quantities. It will keep almost indefinitely in the refrigerator.

CRÊPES

2 eggs	2 T milk
2 T flour	a pinch of salt
1 T cream	

Mix this very smooth; it should be the consistency of thick olive oil. Cook the crêpes in an *iron* 6-inch pan, using a teaspoon of butter for each pancake. Use only enough batter to thin-coat the bottom of the pan; about a tablespoon or two is usually ample. The cooking process requires a deft hand and considerable authority; your first effort may well be depressing, but persevere, and you will quickly get the hang of it!

The crêpes need only a minute or two to brown, then should be quickly flipped over—Henri Charpentier, originator of the recipe, is still (at the age of 80) able to keep *two* iron skillets in operation simultaneously, and to flip his crêpes in the air like a short-order cook with a Western omelette, talking all the while of *la haute cuisine*.

Sauce:

2 oranges	1 tsp orange blossom water
1 lemon	2 ponies each: kirsch, white
4 T vanilla sugar*	curaçao, rum
⅛ lb butter	1 pony maraschino

Cut the orange and lemon peel in julienne strips, and squeeze and strain the juice. Combine with sugar and butter in a pan, bring to a boil. Add orange blossom water and liqueurs; again bring to a boil and remove from fire.

FINAL SERVICE

In a chafing dish, heat enough of the sauce to cover the desired servings (1 cup is ample for serving 4).

Make 3 crêpes per serving. As each crêpe is cooked, fold

* Place a vanilla bean in a pound of granulated sugar, in a tight-capped glass jar, and store for several weeks until sugar is impregnated.

in half and remove to a warm plate. Place the crêpes, three at a time, in the hot sauce. Turn and baste with the hot sauce, fold into quarters and stack around the outside of the chafing dish as you add the next three crêpes. When all have been covered with the sauce, combine 1 pony of each liqueur used in the sauce; add to the chafing dish, heat for 1 minute and flame, turning and twisting the pan so all the crêpes are well coated with the flaming sauce. When the flames die, serve quickly on pre-heated plates.

FROSTED GRAPES (2-Step Cookery)

A blending of chilled fruits with honey, liqueur brandy and sour cream. This dessert must be chilled overnight in order to blend its flavors.

1 pound seedless grapes	2 T each of good Cognac
⅓ cup honey	brandy and lemon juice
	1 pint of sour cream

Wash and pick over the grapes, removing all stems. Place in a serving bowl, pour over the honey, brandy and lemon juice. Mix well and place in the refrigerator. Stir occasionally (before you go to bed, and once or twice in the morning while you are having coffee . . .). Stir again while you are preparing the main dinner courses—and finally place in dessert dishes, topped with a half cup of sour cream for each portion.

MOLASSES CAKE

Lightly spiced and not too rich, this recipe can be put together very rapidly—and left to bake while first courses are served. Serve hot from the oven, with a pitcher of heavy plain cream or a spoonful of vanilla ice cream.

2 T butter	1 T cinnamon
½ cup brown sugar	1 tsp baking soda dissolved
1 egg	in a tablespoon of warm
½ cup molasses	water
½ cup sour cream	1 scant cup of flour

138

Cream butter and sugar together, add beaten egg. Combine baking soda mixture with molasses (never add soda directly to sour cream!) Add molasses to butter-sugar-egg and blend; add cinnamon, sour cream, and finally the sifted flour, mixing thoroughly but not beating too hard. Pour into a greased 6″ square pan and bake in a medium (375) oven for 20 minutes.

APPLE DESSERT

4 large cooking apples, pared, cored and sliced thickly

4 T vanilla sugar

¼ cup butter

6 slices buttered toast, each cut into 3 strips

2 ponies brandy, rum or whiskey

¼ cup melted butter
sugar

Simmer the apple slices in ¼ cup butter, sprinkle with 2 T vanilla sugar, over medium heat until half-cooked. Meanwhile, make the toast, butter it, and cut into strips. Place a third of the toast strips on the bottom of a buttered casserole, cover with half the apples; cover with another third of the toast strips—placed so they are at right angles to the bottom layer—the remainder of the apples, and top with remaining toast strips placed parallel to the ones at the bottom of the dish. Sprinkle with 2 T vanilla sugar and ¼ cup melted butter.

Bake 15 minutes in 400 oven.

Warm the brandy, rum or whiskey (not scotch or gin), flame and pour over the dish before serving.

CHAPTER 14

COFFEE

Coffee is not only universal, but controversial.

It is a strange fact that other people's coffee often seems mysteriously to be more delicious than your own. This is possibly an extension of the basic premise that any meal you did not cook will seem excellent. . . .

There are approximately a hundred ways to make coffee —(yes, there are!)—but there is probably only one way that suits you. Our personal preference is a Chemex—but in the past we have loved percolators . . . and in our extreme youth, we knew how to make delicious boiled coffee with an egg shell!

So the method of making coffee—and the particular blend that suits you—are a very personal matter with which you must cope experimentally. But since a good cup of coffee is distinctively American, this is worthy of your determined experimentation. . . .

Coffee-makers are not exorbitant in price; you can afford to buy several different kinds for personal testing. (The ones you don't like will be enormously helpful when you give a big party!)

Nearly all packaged coffees are similar in price; try one after another, until you find the blend *you* prefer.

Special coffees are a different matter. Generally available is an Italian Espresso coffee. French coffee usually contains a great deal of roasted chicory (in order to stretch the coffee which France does not produce in sufficient quantity), and is therefore slightly bitter.

Turkish coffee is a powder, brewed strong and served *very* sweet in small cups. It can be bought (by mail, if necessary) from Charles & Co., New York City.

CAFE AU LAIT

The true French cafe au lait is a balance of hot milk and strong coffee.

Heat equal parts of milk and heavy cream very gently in a double boiler—1 cup each. Pour the hot cream-milk into one pitcher—and fill a second with fresh strong hot coffee.

Serve by pouring simultaneously from both pitchers into a coffee cup.

MOCHA COFFEE

4 squares bitter cooking chocolate	1 tsp ground cinnamon
	4 cups strong hot coffee

Melt the chocolate and cinnamon in the top of a double boiler; gradually stir in the hot coffee, and distribute among 4 double-sized coffee cups. Serve with sugar and cream.

CAFE ROYALE

This is a do-it-yourself for guests: provide each with a large cup of strong hot black coffee—plus a bouillon spoon containing a lump of sugar, floated in brandy (as much as you can get in the spoon).

Light each spoonful of brandy; hold until the flames die, plunge into cup, then stir until the sugar dissolves.

CAFE DIABLE

An extension of Cafe Royale. This requires a chafing dish. In a heated chafing dish, mix

6 whole cloves	1 stick of cinnamon
2 thin slices of lemon peel and orange peel	6 lumps of sugar
	1½ cups of brandy

Set this afire, and add 4 cups of strong hot coffee.
Stir, and serve (with a ladle) in demi-tasse cups.

As with eggs, every country in the world has its own method of serving coffee.

AUSTRIAN COFFEE

Top each serving of coffee—either iced or hot—with plenty of sweetened whipped cream.

FRENCH COFFEE

The slightly bitter, chicory-impregnated coffee used for a demi-tasse—brew it *double strength* . . . serve in the tiny demi-tasse cups, and *provide a stick of cinnamon instead of a spoon*. Sissies are allowed a lump of sugar—but cream does not go with this coffee.

ITALIAN COFFEE

This, too, is full of chicory. Real Espresso is, literally, distilled via steaming hot water . . . and the machine for making it is truly a wondrous sight, reminiscent of Rube Goldberg.

But the coffee is *good*, though bitter. Roman style, it is served in tiny cups, without sugar or cream, but garnished with a generous curl of lemon peel—and if you never combined lemon with coffee before, try it!

SCANDINAVIAN COFFEE

This is just good strong coffee served with lashings of warmed milk or cream and plenty of sugar—but TURKISH and ARABIAN coffee is entirely different. It should be very hot, frothy and disastrously sweet (unless you are used to it). It is always served in small demi-tasse cups, without sugar or cream.

8 tsp Turkish coffee	4 serving cups of water
8 tsp sugar	(demi-tasse size)

Combine cold water, coffee and sugar in a saucepan and bring it slowly to a boil, stirring until sugar is completely dissolved. It's important to start with cold water and very low heat. . . . When the coffee comes to a boil and begins to froth—remove from the heat and allow the froth to subside. Repeat this operation three times: bringing the coffee to a boil and froth, over low heat, then removing, until the froth subsides. Finally serve quickly, with a little of the froth in each cup.

Yes, it does take time—but they seem to have little else in the Middle East. ∴ . .

COFFEE BLUE DEVIL

Very strong, hot, black coffee, 2 cups

Claret, 1 cup
Sugar, 3 tsp

Use ⅓ wine to ⅔ coffee, and 3 tsps of sugar to every cup of wine.

Combine claret and sugar, bring gently to a boil, add the hot coffee, mix and serve at once in demi-tasse cups.

This coffee was named for the French Alpine soldiers in the First World War.

IRISH COFFEE

Coffee plus whiskey, for a cold winter night. For each serving:

1 jigger Irish whiskey
2 tsp sugar
Strong hot black coffee

Cold whipped or plain heavy cream

Place whiskey and sugar in each cup and stir; fill ¾ full with the hot coffee, stirring until sugar dissolves. Fill to the top with plain or whipped heavy cream.

CHAPTER 15

THE MIDNIGHT SUPPER AND PARTY FARE

The days when a hostess knocked herself out in cleaning and cooking before a gathering of friends are long since gone. Today we give one PARTY a year—perhaps—and consider all the other meetings with friends as completely informal. In either case, the refreshments can achieve a gourmet standard without undue strain.

For end-of-the-evening, whether anticipated or spur of the moment, there are innumerable broiled sandwiches, chafing dish delicacies and

SMORREBROD

The traditional open-faced Danish sandwiches, prepared in advance and chilled until the moment for serving. For these, almost anything goes—provided it is artistically arranged.

No. 1

4 slices pumpernickel bread
4 slices of cold boiled ham
4 slices of liverwurst

radishes, raw carrot, cucumber
butter
Sour cream—½ cup

Butter the pumpernickel; top with ham and center a slice of liverwurst atop the ham. Surround with overlapping slices of radish, cucumber and carrot, and top with a tablespoon of sour cream. Chill before serving.

No. 2

4 slices sweet rye bread, buttered

8 thin slices smoked salmon, fresh cut (not packaged!)

2 T drained capers

½ box whipped cream cheese (small size)

4 T red caviar

4 hard boiled eggs

4 T mayonnaise

1 ripe tomato, peeled and cut in 4 thick slices

Spread buttered sweet rye bread with 2 slices each of smoked salmon, and cover with whipped cream cheese. Place a slice of tomato on each serving; surround with hard boiled egg slices, decorated with red caviar. Top with a tablespoon of mayonnaise, garnished with capers.

No. 3

4 slices buttered white bread

4 slices peeled ripe tomato

8 sardines, drained, boned and split in half

12 anchovy fillets, drained

thin-sliced radishes and cucumber

4 T mayonnaise

4 pickled onions, 4 parsley sprigs

Top bread with a tomato slice, surrounded by thin cucumber slices. Lay 2 opened sardines atop the tomatoes and place a row of overlapping radish slices between them. Place three anchovy fillets at right angles to the sardines. Top with a tablespoon of mayonnaise, decorated with a pickled onion and a tiny sprig of fresh parsley.

No. 4

4 slices of sour rye bread, not buttered

1 pound *finely* ground sirloin steak

½ pound cooked shelled shrimp

4 eggs

2 tsp salt

½ tsp black pepper

1 tsp Worcestershire

1 tsp prepared mustard

2 T lemon juice

Combine lemon juice, mustard, Worcestershire, pepper, salt and finely ground steak, and mix very very thoroughly with your hands. This should take at least 5 minutes—or

145

someone will get a hot mouthful of seasoning that you have failed to distribute properly!

Spread a quarter pound of the beef mixture on each slice of bread.

Make a slight depression in the center of each Smørrebrød, and in it carefully place a *raw* egg. Surround this with cooked shrimps, and sprinkle with a little freshly ground black pepper.

This is the Danish version of Tartar Steak—but you will make it yourself as you mix the raw egg with raw steak and shrimps on your own plate. Yes, it's *good;* smear it around and eat it.

Anything at all is useful for Smørrebrød: leftover meats, thinly sliced, or bits of vegetable salads; ham or bacon, cold fish slices or caviar. All that is necessary is to prepare the sandwiches with an eye to beauty; chill—and serve with plenty of hot coffee at midnight.

Broiled sandwiches are equally simple, to be prepared on a baking sheet for insertion beneath electric grill or gas flame.

SIMPLE SIMONS

4 slices white bread	Various decorations: shrimps,
½ pound soft cheddar cheese	or bacon slices, ham bits,
2 T Worcestershire Sauce	or sweet pickle slices, etc.,
1 T Bahamian mustard	etc.

Cream together cheese, Worcestershire and mustard; spread carefully to cover every bit of the bread. Decorate each slice with cooked shrimps, bacon bits, or what have you. Broil about 5 minutes, until cheese browns and bubbles.

CHEESE is one of the great standbys for a gourmet chef . . . useful in every possible service course either in combination or to stand alone in all its dignity.

All cheeses have their own uses, but pasteurized, processed, "cheese foods," commercial cheese dips, and so on cannot meet the standards of a real gourmet. People who live in cities boasting a good imported cheese shop are (for

146

nce) better off than the people in small communities who must depend entirely on what's available in the local supermarket—but it is still wise to know what to buy, and how to serve it.

Roquefort, Gorgonzola, Bleu and Stilton are the blue-veined rich crumbly cheeses of France, Italy, Denmark and England. There are differences in taste, of course, but in general, any one of these may be substituted for any other.

Port du Salut, Bel Paese, Oka are French, Italian and Canadian versions of a basic soft creamy-yellow cheese. *Pont l'Eveque* is a slightly sharper member of this family.

Camembert, Brie and Poona are French and American cheeses, which are supposed to be ripened to an exact consistency, of half-melted butter. The high point of any gourmet's existence is a perfectly ripened Camembert! It cannot be achieved with a pasteurized brand. The cheese should be soft to the point that it literally drips and runs onto the plate. Gourmets often eat it, rind and all. Brie and Poona also should be soft, but are never supposed to be as liquid as Camembert.

Edam, Gouda, Provolone, Pineapple, Cheddar and Swiss are the firm Dutch, Italian, English and Swiss cheeses, usually forming the backbone of any cheese board. Although their flavors differ, nearly everyone likes them. *Muenster* is softer in texture, but equally mild-flavored.

Crème Chantilly and Hablé are usually classed as dessert cheeses, because they are soft and sufficiently full-flavored to serve by themselves.

Finally, there are the smelly cheeses: *Limburger, Liederkranz and Sap Sago,* respectively German, American and Norwegian. And they definitely *smell,* although delicious if one develops a palate for them.

In addition, of course, there are many other imported cheeses, such as the caraway-seed Scandinavian types and various local European cheeses such as a fine Neuchatel. You should know, also, that there are two varieties of Swiss cheese —the one with the holes is actually termed Emmenthaler, but far more delicious (and much more difficult to obtain!) is the true Gruyère, which has no holes and possesses a special nut-like flavor. Bloomingdale's Food department, at Lexington and 59th Street in New York, stocks *real* imported Gruyère.

For a midnight cheese tray, then a real gourmet would offer a selection of the imported cheese, flanked with pumpernickel, rye bread, crisp crackers . . . but there are other things to be done with cheese.

CHEESE FONDUE and WELSH RABBIT

Cheese Fondue is the national Swiss dish. It differs from the Welsh Rabbit we have known, and loved so long, only in using Swiss cheese rather than Cheddar, and white wine in place of beer. A Fondue is prepared over hot water, either in a double boiler or a chafing dish.

1 pound Swiss cheese, grated or finely cubed	2 T Kirsch liqueur
½ bottle dry white wine	¼ tsp nutmeg
½ clove garlic, pressed	½ tsp salt
2 T butter	¼ tsp black pepper

Add garlic to wine and bring to a boil over hot water; add cheese and stir until it melts. Add butter, nutmeg, salt and pepper, stirring constantly until very smooth and well blended. Finally, add the Kirsch and serve at once, accompanied by toast strips or crusty French bread.

The only trick to this dish is to keep the pan of cheese-wine mixture well surrounded by hot water, so it blends smoothly. The cheese *must* be imported Emmenthaler or Gruyère; processed, pasteurized or domestic Swiss will not produce a proper Fondue.

The traditional service of a Fondue is from a common pot or casserole placed in the center of the table. There are special fondue forks, which are long 2-tined spears, but ordinary dinner forks will suffice. Each guest places a toast square or bit of French bread on the fork and dips it into the fondue dish (which is kept over warm water), sops up as much melted cheese as possible and eats with gusto.

THE WELL BELOVED RABBIT

This is basically an English dish. While the British are supposed not to be able to cook, it is a matter of fact that they have still produced a great many definitive gourmet-standard delicacies . . . Yorkshire pudding, Roast Beef, Stilton and Cheddar cheese, and *Welsh Rabbit*, which is a hearty combination of melted Cheddar cheese with stale beer or ale.

The proper way to make a Welsh Rabbit is to open a bottle of beer or ale several hours, even a full day, in advance; to retain a cupful—and bestow the rest upon your thirsty husband or beau. This is one reason men like Welsh Rabbits.

1 pound of the *sharpest*, rat-trap, store cheese available, cut in small cubes
2 T butter
1 cup *stale* beer or ale

1 tsp dry mustard
1 tsp paprika
Plenty of toast, some buttered and some plain

Melt butter, add finely diced sharp cheese, place over hot water and stir until cheese begins to melt. Add beer or ale gradually, stirring smooth; add mustard and paprika, and stir until cheese is completely melted and smooth. Serve over hot buttered toast, with unbuttered toast fingers to mop up remaining plate sauce.

The perfect Welsh Rabbit must be served and eaten while *hot*, or it will become "stringy." If you can obtain a soft unpasteurized Cheddar cheese, the possibility of stringiness will diminish . . . But there is no substitute for the plain sharp American store cheese, when it comes to flavor.

A GOLDEN BUCK is simply the Welsh Rabbit sauce topped by a poached egg for each portion . . . and a YORKSHIRE BUCK adds two strips of crisp cooked bacon to a Golden Buck (In case you had wondered . . .).

For a midnight snack, the chafing dish is indispensable, and much can be done with it. A long way back in this book (we have forgotten the exact page) we pointed out that even the most ravenous guests will control themselves if they can watch the food being cooked.

Aside from the great traditional cheese dishes, there are such midnight gastronomic titbits as

MUSHROOMS FLAMBÉ—or mushrooms in a rich cream sauce on toast

1 pound mushrooms (caps only—save the stems for another day)	¼ cup brandy
	½ cup heavy cream, heated off-stage
¼ cup butter	8 pieces of toast, unbuttered
1 cup dry sherry	a dash of salt

Melt butter in a chafing dish, add mushroom caps and saute until lightly browned. Add sherry and simmer violently, until the pan is nearly dry. Meanwhile make the toast slices and keep warm. Add the brandy to the mushrooms, flame with a lighted match, and shake the pan until flames die. Finally, stir in the warm cream, season with salt, and serve on the toast triangles.

PARTY FARE

Everybody loves a party.

Parties are a woman's chore; a great many women work —or they are lazy—or they don't know how. . . .

This is why there are so few real parties nowadays . . . but it doesn't have to be that way, because it's quite possible to give a buffet supper party for 40 people without undue strain.

All that is needed is about three free hours the previous evening—and not all of them will be devoted to cooking!

SWEDISH MEATBALLS (2-Step Cookery)

2 eggs	3 T fresh chopped parsley
6 slices white bread	1 T salt
1 cup milk	1 T Worcestershire Sauce
6 T onions	½ tsp black pepper
6 T butter	¼ tsp dry mustard
1 lb chopped beef	¼ cup butter ⎤
⅓ lb chopped veal	¼ cup flour ⎦ —for cooking
⅓ lb chopped pork	1 pint sour cream

Step #1:

Soak bread in milk; saute onion in butter for 3 minutes; beat eggs slightly. Squeeze excess milk from bread, combine all ingredients and work with your hands—mixing and squeezing everything together.

You must mix for no less than a full *five minutes* by the kitchen timer! This is a tiresome job, but essential in order to blend thoroughly, and create the smooth texture required.

Form the mixture into 48 small balls; lay them on a large platter covered with waxed paper, in layers, and finally cover the whole dish with waxed paper. Store overnight in the refrigerator.

Step #2:

Warm the meatballs to room temperature before cooking —which only means "when you get home from the office, take the meatballs out of the icebox!" Let them *sit*, while you get dressed for the party, receive the guests and serve drinks and canapes.

Twenty minutes before dinner time, dust the meatballs with flour (by sprinkling a ¼ cup of flour through a sieve over the meatballs—or by gently tossing them a few at a time, in a brown paper bag of plain flour).

Cook in ¼ cup melted butter, very gently for about 15 minutes, turning occasionally to brown. Cover with the sour cream and let stand for 5 minutes (covered in the pan, with heat turned off). The cream will curdle—do not despair; it is supposed to!

BAKED BEANS

For a Buffet of 20 people . . . but quarter the recipe for home consumption. This is 2-Step cookery, but extremely simple.

4 *large* tins baked beans
(*without* tomato sauce)
4 large onions, thin sliced
1 cup molasses
1 cup brown sugar
¼ cup Worcestershire Sauce
1 T baking soda dissolved in
2 T water and added to
molasses

½ cup soluble coffee crystals
2 cups Bourbon
½ cup dry mustard
hot water as required
6 tins Vienna sausage,
drained

Step #1:

Combine beans, onions, mustard, molasses and soda, brown sugar, Worcestershire in a shallow bowl. Sprinkle the soluble coffee crystals over the top (undissolved); add the Bourbon liquor, and very gently turn and mix until all ingredients are incorporated. Cover and store overnight.

Step #2:

Stir-mix the beans thoroughly; top with the Vienna sausages and place the casserole in a hot (400) oven for 30 minutes.

BUFFET SALAD (2-Step Cookery)

Easiest of all party salads is the Vegetable Combination . . . which needs only a few minutes to prepare, before chilling overnight in the refrigerator until serving time. For 20 people, you will need. . . .

4 boxes frozen mixed vegetables	4 T minced fresh parsley
4 cold boiled potatoes, peeled and diced	4 or more tomatoes (depending on size) peeled and quartered
1 bunch of radishes	Green and black olives
1 bunch of scallions	8 hardboiled eggs: 4 for garnishing, and 4 coarsely cut
1 green pepper, seeded	
4 large stalks of celery, coarsely cut	1 or 2 heads of iceberg lettuce (depending on size)
4 peeled raw carrots, cut in slender sticks	2 cups mayonnaise dressing
1 large white onion, grated	1 cup milk
	½ cup pot cheese (optional)

Step #1:

Boil potatoes in their jackets for 20 minutes or until tender-*firm*. Blanch frozen vegetable packages, by placing in hot water and cooking about 10 minutes. Vegetables should be very *firm* and underdone.

Wash and coarsely cut radishes, celery, scallions, and green pepper. Peel and quarter tomatoes; scrape and thin-slice carrots.

Combine radishes, celery, scallions and pepper with drained vegetables; chill overnight in a covered bowl. Store peeled tomato sections and boiled potatoes (peeled) in separate bowls to chill overnight.

MAYONNAISE DRESSING

Combine mayonnaise with milk, adding slowly and stirring until thin and smooth. Add grated onion, minced parsley and pot-cheese. The dressing should be extremely thin, so that it will pour and distribute itself easily over all the vegetables. Store overnight in a covered bowl.

Step #2:

(For final serving)
Dice cold potatoes and 4 shelled hard boiled eggs, and add to main vegetable bowl.

Vigorously stir up the dressing, adding more milk if it

seems not thin enough (it should be the consistency of Half and Half). Pour dressing over vegetables and mix gently but thoroughly, until everything is coated—but do not mash or break up any of the vegetable bits!

Line a very large salad bowl with the big lettuce leaves, spreading them to curl up about the top; place coarse-cut lettuce in the bottom of the bowl. Pour the mixed vegetables on top—and decorate with tomato wedges, carrot fingers, olives and 4 quartered hard boiled eggs . . . plus fresh parsley sprigs or watercress.

BUFFET SHRIMPS

An alternate hot dish for a buffet, to be teamed with Swedish meatballs or Baked Beans. Quarter the recipe and prepare it in a chafing dish for a midnight poker party. . . .

4 lbs cooked shelled shrimps	⅓ cup ground dill seed
4 cans condensed mushroom soup	2 cups slivered almonds, toasted in 3 T butter or olive oil
3 cups light cream	
1 T salt	8 cups cooked rice

For a buffet party of 20 people:

Place 2 quarts of water in a deep sauce pot, add ½ cup butter and 2 T salt. When it boils, add 8 cups quick-cooking rice. Stir well, cover tightly, remove from heat, and set aside to mature.

Heat condensed soup, thinned with cream over hot water; add salt and ground dill. When thoroughly heated, add shelled shrimps, and continue to heat until ready to serve.

Toast almond slivers in butter or olive oil, shaking the pan until well browned. Add to the shrimps, just before serving.

Serve the shrimp-almond mixture in a buffet deep-dish placed over a warmer, with rice at the side . . . but this sort of dish is always better if the host or hostess serves it personally, in which case the toasted almonds should be in a separate dish, and sprinkled atop the final serving of rice topped by shrimps in dill sauce . . .

154

157

158

159